Principles of a Brilliant Life

A Lifestyle Guide for Urban Professionals

Woody Smith

Principles of a Brilliant Life: A Lifestyle Guide for Urban Professionals

Print ISBN 978-1-941071-51-9
ebook ISBN 978-1-941071-52-6

STAIRWAY PRESS—LAS VEGAS

Cover Design by Guy D. Corp
www.GrafixCorp.com

STAIRWAY≡PRESS

www.StairwayPress.com
848 North Rainbow Blvd #5015
Las Vegas, NV 89107 USA

Acknowledgements

**Your work is to discover your world and then
with all your heart give yourself to it.**
—Buddha

THE BEST TEACHERS in my life didn't try to fill
me with facts or make me think in predetermined
patterns. They gave me tools for thinking; taught me
how to find the needed information and develop the
processes required to solve the problem.

I dedicate this book to George "Easy" Anner who
taught me to think logically and multi-prospectively and
to my mother who taught me to dream. I also dedicate
this book to my wife—Eileen—who stood beside me on
this journey and helped me find the right questions. She
also helped me rebuild the bonfire of "wonder" and the
desire to "look behind the curtain" at what is really going
on. And even more importantly she taught me to always
enjoy the trip and don't take yourself too seriously.

Introduction

OSCAR WILDE SAID:

I put my genius in my life and my talent in my career.

That is truth! Wilde realized that every one of us has the genius needed to build a wonderful life. Careers, on the other hand, are not that simple. Successful careers are the product of education, opportunity, luck, training and perhaps some special ability (like Tiger Woods, J. S. Bach or Albert Einstein). Careers (with or without "special" skills) are only partially controllable, because, in reality, they're controlled by society, chance and possibly: fate.

Maybe an example will clarify what I'm trying to say. Let's suppose you just landed a great job at a great company with a wonderful history of growth and stability. Your future looks bright, and hopefully it will be, but do you have any real control? The company could be bought or declare bankruptcy. Your boss could see you as a threat to his position.

Hidden factors you cannot anticipate or control will always exist. No matter how skillfully you manage your career, things will happen that you can't predict. Unforeseeable, external forces control the game.

Consider this bit of weird history, Betamax (video coding format) was technically and visually a better product than VHS, yet VHS won out. Why? Obviously, no single cause determined the outcome, but history now shows that the single biggest factor was the pornography industry's adoption of the VHS format.

Go figure!

It would have taken a true psychic to have foreseen that possibility. What I'm saying is; that success in your chosen career path is not in your control. You can make completely rational and correct decisions all along your path and still lose if you're only focused on the outcome. Or you can make terrible decisions and never suffer a single mishap. A key question: if you can't control or strongly influence the final result, how smart is it to base your identity and life on your career? Some people have a real talent for building a successful career path and have the luck to go with it. Other people may have even more talent, but considerably less luck. It's a crapshoot and you won't know how it's going to work out until it's over.

Many of us today have fallen into the trap of building our life around our work. If you had asked your parents what they wanted for you when you were born, do you think they would have even mentioned a career? They would probably have said something about being happy and successful. And those words happy and successful, I can assure you, had nothing to do with work. I had the good fortune to discuss this topic with my father when he was in his late 70s and I was truly surprised by his response. I always viewed my father as a success-driven man. He was a fighter pilot in World War II who graduated from law school and med school upon his return to civilian life. Tremendous opportunities presented themselves to him, but he turned them all down because, during those years, my brother and I were born, and to him that was the focus of his life and he wasn't going to compromise his family for his career.

In the end, he had a wonderfully successful career, but more importantly, he lived a successful life. He was active in politics and built a successful legal practice specializing in medical law. Later in his career he became a judge, but he never missed attending one of my sporting events or my brother's band concerts and that's what he was really proud of. He loved the law, but the practice of law was not what defined him as a man.

My father was still a proud man at the end of his life even though his abilities—both physical and mental—had deteriorated because of health problems. He had a very positive view of himself to the end of his life because it was based on his "human-ness' not on his skills or accomplishments. Dad saw himself as the man he really was and that gave him an innate pride based on having lived his beliefs through his service as a citizen and a father. I find myself crying as I write these words. My mother and father gave me some great gifts, but the greatest gift was the example of how to live life with integrity.

Sadly, I didn't remember this message until the roof fell in on me. I had always viewed my father (and my mother because of her support of my father's actions) as a success-driven man, and from my perspective success meant accomplishing the goals I set for myself in the business world. I couldn't have been more wrong. My father had plenty of career successes, and he enjoyed them—the whole family enjoyed them—but they didn't define him. Somehow, I picked up the wrong message about the meaning of success (happiness equals career success). Strangely, my brother, who grew up in the same environment with the same examples, got my father's and mother's message correct.

Hmmmmmm....

Luckily for you and me, everyone is born with the special genius necessary for a brilliant life if he or she takes the time to discover it. And luckily for you and me, you can do it at any point in your life.

It can't be learned from a book alone, but I can recommend several books to help you on this journey [see Appendix A]. This book is my attempt to simplify the process of self-discovery into a set of concrete procedures I have found useful on this journey. I have developed them for my own reflections, from psychology and philosophy books and courses I've taken, and from working with my fellow journeyers in my process group. These procedures will get you to the right place to start this journey and give you tools that will help guide you along the way.

As it was written on a bathroom stall in the engineering building at Penn State:

The journey of 1000 miles begins with a single, 'Oh shit! Where's my car keys!?'

The most important thing you should know about this book:

the tools are excellent, but...
...their real genius lies in their application!

Each person's life is unique, so each application of these tools will be unique. Learn the techniques, live the techniques, but don't be afraid to modify them for yourself.

Contents

Know Yourself

MOST OF MY life on this "turn of the wheel" I didn't see any advantage in self-reflection. Then, at age forty, something changed—me. I realized my life direction wasn't what I had envisioned when I was eighteen years old. So, I spent the next several months examining my life in humbling and frightening detail This self-examination made me run (not walk) back in the direction of the status quo. Ah, safety...like a drowning man, I grasped anything that floated by to maintain the illusion of progress—not floundering. First I grabbed onto spirituality, but not as a means of building a solid base for a quality life, but as a way of rationalizing my previous decisions.

Let me explain what I mean; I grew up in a Midwestern, Methodist home in a safe, supportive, success-oriented (I thought back then) environment. Without a word being said, I knew the secret to a happy life. The psychological environment and social systems I was born into "guaranteed" a happy life. And all I had to do was completely buy into the party line. Just act, talk, think and behave like everyone else. Deep thinking, reflection and individuality were neither desired or permitted. I didn't have to worry about what to believe, how to act or with whom I should associate. By the age of twelve, I had a "complete" sense of identity: a belief system, a moral code, a world perspective and a well-defined set of life goals. My top three goals were money, happiness and procreation.

Read the last section again. Count the hidden assumptions. How many do you count?

- The most obvious one is the purpose of life is to be happy [Happy, Happy! Joy, Joy!]. Happy is good, but is it really the central purpose, meaning and goal of life?
- A second hidden assumption is that chaos and complexity are bad.
- The third hidden assumption is that pain and anxiety must be completely and totally avoided—which is Absolutely False!

I frequently encounter such hidden assumptions in my process group and the affects can severely limit anyone trying to live a full, vibrant life.

The last hidden assumption I want to discuss is the message society embeds in our subconscious minds. Society wants you to believe that conforming to its rules is essential to a happy, productive life.

What do I mean when I say "society?" Just think of it as the "establishment"—whatever works for you. The over-arching purpose of all social processes, as far as I can determine, is propagation of the species. And the principle process that ensures successful propagation is strict social control. Some social critics have suggested that all human advancement is produced by people who ignore some but not all the restrictions placed on them by society. My version of that statement is:

All human advancement is produced by people who selectively ignore certain societal restrictions while maintaining the appearance of conforming.

To deviate willfully from socially determined norms and rules is to invite societal backlash unless or until you become successful—in a socially acceptable manner, of course.

Deep. But is it useful? It's tremendously useful once you internalize the truth that society sees you merely as a tool to work its will. You must awaken yourself to the realization that you are embedded in a meta-system (a system of systems) with goals that are totally its own, not yours. The good news is many of society's goals are congruent with yours, but how will you know which ones until you read, think and reflect? Otherwise, you must either completely buy in or completely reject it. Either way, society completely controls you.

Here are some questions to consider:

- What are your life goals?
- What do you think society's goals are for you?
- How do your life goals match up with society's?

Sadly, you'll need to do this quite regularly, because society and your goals will change. Sometimes suddenly. The flow of life is long periods of no change...and then—Boom!—comes massive change. Sometimes you and society will change at the same time, but usually it will be you who experience a sudden, irrevocable change that will leave your head spinning.

MEGA HINT

You need to re-evaluate your role in society within the context of this new change. Ask yourself how will this affect your relationships with family, friends, work and your self image?

You must do this every time a major change happens in your life. I believe you will be shocked by how much you had previously taken your role in society for granted.

HINT

Don't confuse information with knowledge. We live in a world flooded with flashy information that masquerades as knowledge and wisdom—it isn't! Knowledge and wisdom comes from careful consideration of all pertinent information before drawing a conclusion.

HINT

Cultivate a variety of sources. Talk to family, friends, professors, monks, ministers, and rabbis. Drink deeply of books and the Internet. Approach this task as if your life depends on it.

SUPER MEGA HINT

Make sure your heart and mind agree on all your beliefs—this is the central precept of neurolinguistic programming!!!

Dig deep when your mind and emotions conflict. Spent some real effort understanding where these conflicting internal views originate. Meditate, pray, or reflect on your choices—do the work! Here are some questions to ask yourself:

- Why have you allowed these conflicts to exist within yourself?
- What purposes might these conflicts serve?
- What other feelings, behaviors or attitudes did you have

to modify, change or repress to allow this internal contradiction?

Don't worry about the exact point in time or the triggering event that caused you to develop a mind/body dichotomy because psychologically you will revisit this nexus point many times until you heal this split. Some people talk about this as "unfinished business," "soul splintering," "repression," or as a "coping mechanism." Whatever! However, they all agree that the psychological effect effectively traps part of yourself in the past. And, maintaining these internal contradictions actively limits your worldview, your opportunities and your emotional range. If you don't resolve these conflicts, you'll find yourself continually revisiting them. Is it worth it? You know the answer.

Many people before me have made this point, but I believe Sun Tzu said it best. My interpretation of his words is:

> *...you can't control the world (don't try), but by knowing yourself, you will have the maximum number of options available to you in any situation. Self-knowledge, planning, flexibility and intelligent information gathering give you a massive advantage for influencing the outcome of any situation.*

This isn't some psycho, spiritual, vision quest thing. "Knowing yourself" in this context is not about giving yourself an "unfair" advantage in life; it's about seeing yourself without illusions. It's also great from a psychological and spiritual standpoint.

What should you know about yourself?

What are your passions? Ask yourself what you really want to do. Are you living that life now? Probably not, unless you have taken the time to develop and follow a well thought-out plan. The big question is then how to develop a plan to allow you to follow your dreams? This is a tough but essential journey. It requires real commitment, and you need to start now.

The first step to knowing yourself is documenting your priorities and goals. Write them down and sort them out later. Dream big! Put timeframes on each of them. Think about what you want next month, next year and in next decade. Write them down. Don't edit and don't judge. Don't worry about being organized or writing in full sentences or even full thoughts. And don't tell anyone else you're doing this.

I ask you not to tell anyone because modern human beings are embedded in multiple, overlapping social systems that have their own goals for you. Family, friends and co-workers can unknowingly impose their values and goals on you without concern for *your* values and goals. As part of the process of developing your goals and values you need to spend some time actively reflecting, meditating or praying on what this multifaceted social system expects of you versus what you expect of yourself.

You can't possibly be cognizant of all the factors and the ones you are aware of will—most likely—be partially ambiguous. That's not really important—what's really important is identifying the key factors within your present dynamic. Try to be as complete and clear as possible when identifying all the factors, but don't stress too much about them. Spend the bulk of your time identifying and understanding the key factors.

Questions:

- What is central to your life right now?
- What things are you ignoring? Why?
- What are you most passionate about?
- How do these things relate to your goals?
- Is a life transition about to happen?
- How can you order your life to avoid useless pain?
- How do you balance your needs versus those of the people around you?

KEY POINT

Write this stuff down. Don't wait. Do it now!

If I have a problem remembering what I did last week, how can I expect to remember all the details months or years later? Writing things down allows you to dynamically track your beliefs and goals over an extended period of time. Core beliefs probably won't change, but you might see interesting nuances develop as your life changes and grows. This should be a living record of your hopes, dreams and beliefs. Make it speak to you.

My favorite philosophers, Nietzsche and Wittgenstein, were brilliant men, but they couldn't write worth a plugged nickel. To ensure everyone understood the things they felt were important, they often repeated things three times. I do the same thing in my journal (and this book).

Make lists, draw diagrams, put dates on everything and re-read your writings regularly!

Add and subtract from it as needed—make it a living record of the great project that is your life. Add pictures, poetry and include your favorite books and movies. Record the transitions, the highs and lows. Tracking your goals and progress will be massively rewarding.

Understanding how you process information, knowing what you believe, and deciding where you want to go doesn't have to be a complicated process. Most people are unclear on these three questions only because they never spend any time searching for their answers.

This part of the journey to yourself isn't about fixing your faults. This part of the journey is about documenting and accepting the person you are today. Don't get sidetracked—stay on mission. Spend time recording the facts and events of your life and don't waste valuable time interpreting, rationalizing or mitigating any of it. Record the good, the bad and the ugly.

History that shaped you and you need to accept that if you want to evolve and grow.

It's time to loop back and rethink your relationship to your external (society, family and work) and internal self-presentations to clarify how they affect your view of yourself. I've already covered this topic, but I want to talk about it again, because if you have done the thinking and recording of your feelings, beliefs and insights, you probably have a different perspective now. You need to revisit the relationship you have with your mind, body and spirit. Do this regularly and record your thinking and you will happily shocked. Add stories—both the mundane and the glorious—there are plenty of both in your life.

How do you present yourself to the world? More importantly, how do you present yourself to yourself? I'm not one of those who are going to tell you that your public face/persona is unimportant because it is important, but not as important as the face/persona you see yourself from your internal perspective. It's this internal perspective (the "me") that is key to living a fulfilling, mindful and balanced life. It would be great if your external life could display a balance of body, mind and spirit but it's not likely to happen because you have limited control and influence over your external world; however, your internal world can be, and should be, highly controllable if you follow the techniques in this book.

It's also highly desirable that your socially perceived personality, your persona, be compatible with your life situation if you want to minimize the stress of internal versus external self image. For best results, your social persona should be flexible, adaptive and congruent with your beliefs and ideals. I also hope other people perceive your persona as encompassing all the positive attributes and values of your social group. The external appearance of conformity—your camouflage—will give you the greatest amount of slack. A strong, balanced persona is a useful tool, but it can cause you major problems if you allow yourself to become completely identified with it and forget your true self—the part of you that you and you alone, see, feel and know. It's this part you have complete control over. And it's this part that's going to determine the quality of your life. In our modern world we spend a lot of time "dressing up" our external, public face when we should be balancing and enlarging, completing and optimizing our internal life.

With limited time and society's incessant white noise, you will always be tempted to spend most of your time on externals, but life's biggest gains come from a more balanced approach. The techniques of intention, time management, budgeting and planning are essential to this process. These techniques will generate the time, space and opportunity you need to address both the external and the internal aspects of your life. And by utilizing the other skills you will learn from this book—self-awareness, non-judgment, a phenomenological perspective, the "cycle of awareness" and the "TOTE"[1] methodology, you will develop an internal balance of body mind and spirit.

These techniques are key elements to developing an internal synergistic self perspective. Is this important? Yes, because synergistic processes allow each element (thinking, feeling, reasoning, intuition, etc.) to take the lead when it is necessary and then recede when it's no longer needed. Our internal life should be a synergistic process. The purpose of life's journey is to develop this synergistic system of mind, body and spirit.

---

[1] Test-Operate-Test-Exit method described later.

KEY POINT

I started this book with this topic because I want you to read this book from the perspective of trying to understand how these techniques can help you build a synergistic internal life.

KEY POINT

I started this book with this topic because I want you to read this book from the perspective of trying to understand how these techniques can help you build a synergistic internal life.

KEY POINT

I started this book with this topic because I want you to read it from the perspective of understanding how these techniques can help you build a synergistic, balanced internal life that will produce success in your external life.

A SUMMARY OF THE JOURNEY TO YOURSELF

- The journey begins with acceptance and self-knowledge.
  - List and prioritize your goals
  - Document this journey.
- Talk to the significant others in your life
  - Consider going on a retreat.
- Spend time regularly doing this; don't wait for major transitions.
  - Avoid judgment.
- Everything in life is change
  - Be open to change.

- Beliefs
- Goals
- Roles
- Don't be Mr. Fix-It
- Develop a balance between the external and internal
- Understand your relationship to the big three:
    - Mind
    - Body
    - Spirit
- Conscious
- Subconscious
- Physical
- Emotional
- Primal
- Build your synergy
    - Which aspect is dominating now?
    - Why?
    - What changes can I make to improve the balance?
- The journey to yourself is never-ending
- Give yourself credit
- Enjoy the journey

Meaning and Living in the Present

BEFORE WE GET into the meat of this chapter, let me define a couple of terms. First, let me share with you my definition of the word "meaning". Originally, this Latin/Greek word meant "to weigh."

Because of the subjective nature of meaning, I think it is still the best way to define it. Second, how do I define the word "gestalt"? This German word lacks a precise English equivalent. So I end up using many English words to equal one German word. A gestalt is: a whole, a configuration, a pattern with a cohesive relationship among its parts such that the subjective meaning is derived from the relationship of the parts to one other and that this meaning is of greater significance than the sum of the individual parts.

I advise you to memorize these definitions. You'll need them.

All right, the academic part of the chapter is over. Now, I want to talk about something that initially shocked me. But before I explain, let me ask you a question: how would you like to multiply the effectiveness of your life, by, say, 500%? You can make that happen, but it will require you to change your relationship to yourself and to the world around you. I'm not kidding. You can improve your life by a factor of 5 with a simple change. I feel safe in predicting you'll find that you will sleep better, concentrate better and improve your memory. Your self-esteem and self-image will be tremendously improved, too. And this simple technique is called Living with Awareness.

"Living with awareness", or as some say, "living in the now" is not a cure-all that will solve all your problems, but it will greatly improve your awareness of yourself and your life, which is the necessary first step. The process of "Living with Awareness" is a synthesis of most of the techniques that we will discuss in this book. It's a philosophy of life, of living mindfully. It's an attitude of acceptance that eliminates expectations. It's a commitment to living your beliefs. It's also about the power of intention and "will" to resist sliding into the "blue zone" when things go wrong. It's about living with an integrated, wholistic perspective. I coin the term *wholistic* to capture something grander more inclusive than *holistic*.

What do I mean by wholistic perspective? My interpretation of a wholistic perspective is that it is an integration of mind and body, past and future, goals and dreams and damn near everything else. It's easiest to understand from an example. Let's suppose you're talking to a dear friend who is going through some bad times and who is not very happy with you either. And let's further suppose this friend is not very good at communicating. Here's this person you love standing in front of you in pain who believes that you are a source of at least some of the pain. As a person "living in the now," how should you approach this situation?

The first thing you would have to do is fully accept the present situation as its given (stay in moment. don't interpret.) and have no expectations for the outcome of this confrontation. The first half of the previous sentence—acceptance—I found I was reasonably good at pretty quickly, but the second half of the sentence is still a challenge for me to this day. The importance of doing this can't be overstated. It finally dawned upon me a few years ago that I wasn't able to completely eliminate expectations but I could minimize them and move them closer to the end of the process. And that's all I really needed to do.

The mental processes involved in forming expectations remove you from being present with the other person at the crucial moment of any discussion—the beginning. Speaking for myself, I usually attempt to express my most pressing feelings and needs at the beginning of any discussion. If I'm lucky I will repeat these wants and needs several more times during the discussion, but not necessarily. Many times I wander off into other topics and become frustrated because I perceive other people do not understand what I'm trying to say to them; likewise, they often didn't understand me because they are off forming expectations, too.

Secondly, you need to drop your defensiveness at the outset of the discussion. Deep, slow breathing is a wonderful help. Stay present because, if you're off reviewing the past history of your relationship as it applies to this present situation, you will not be present with your friend. You have to adopt the position of interested observer until you've completely heard your friend out. And, as you're listening, you shouldn't be building your psychic defenses against what your friend is saying. You must put aside your judgment of what your friend is saying because it is their truth—realistic or not.

KEY POINT

You need to not only see and hear your friends; you must feel their emotions.

Personally, I use to find it tough to keep my mouth shut and listen mindfully, but because it is absolutely essential, I learned. So can you! I found it even tougher to try to hear and feel their emotions while silencing my own, but I did. Avoiding pre-judgment was difficult to learn, but after I saw how much it improved my communications and enriched my understanding, it became a snap. Intellectually I had always known that I had trouble expressing what I was really thinking and feeling; I also was aware that most people have similar problems. But, without a commitment to living in the now and being present with the people in front of me, it was just an irrelevant piece of intellectual knowledge. However, if you're mindfully living in the present, you will be aware of how you are affecting other people so you can tailor your communication to maximize their understanding.

Now, after you've given your full attention to your friends, allow yourself to take a few extra, deep, relaxed, breaths in order to hear them fully. Before you turn to the task of evaluating reach out with all your senses to determine whether they've completed this part of their communication or not. If this phase of their communication to you is complete, check in to see where you're at—mentally and physically. I hope you were mindfully aware of everything involving you and your friends, but it is always good to monitor yourself before you start speaking. Never speak before you're ready. Don't suffer from premature verbal ejaculation.

Maybe it's time to ask some clarifying questions or share your observations, but avoid making judgments at this point. Let this phase of communication continue until both of you have reached a stopping point.

Sometimes all it takes to solve the problem is authentic listening; other times it may require action on your part or on the part of both of you. Any required action should focus on the present situation, while being sensitive to the complete history of your overall relationship and not just the present disagreement. And, after you have completed the necessary actions, allow yourself to withdraw, relax and complete the experience.

Here's the key point: do everything you agreed to do but don't get attached to the expectation that the other person will do what they were asked to do. Don't let the trap of expectations control you. You can only control yourself. You can show the other person possible alternatives to what they currently believe and do, but you can't make them believe or act differently. Don't even try.

Let's take a moment to revisit an earlier point. I'm sure you have noticed the majority of your communications tend to repeat. This can happen because we lose track of what we are saying, or because we perceive that the other person doesn't understand what we are saying, or because what you're saying isn't what you mean. Many times we repeat ourselves because we feel that the other person isn't feeling what we're trying to express emotionally This will definitely be true if they're judging what you're saying or considering what they are going to say instead of listening...

KEY POINT

In many conversations, emotions are more important than the topic itself. Listen for the emotions as well as the facts. (I know, I'm repeating myself.)

Have you spent any time thinking about how human beings generate meaning and how that affects our ability to communicate? Since we haven't evolved to the point of using telepathy to communicate brain-to-brain, we are forced to use the limited vehicles of language, symbolism and custom.

I've spent a lot of time thinking, reading, and reflecting on these topics to help me understand my style of communicating. Clearly, an in-depth discussion of these topics is outside the intended purpose of this book; however, I think it's important that I sketch out a serviceable mental model of how I believe we generate meaning so you can understand my perspective and hopefully have some insight into your process of meaning making. A group of German psychologists in the 1930s developed a theory of how we construct meaning from visual inputs. They were collectively known as Gestalt psychologists.

Typically, the English translation of "gestalt" talks about it as a wholeness, a bold figure against a featureless background. The figure in a gestalt is comprised of all the elements involved in a central need or emotion of the present moment. How the figure is structured/assembled (using memories, external inputs, beliefs and perception) is, in their theory, is how we make meaning.

Upon first discovering this theory, I thought I'd found the ultimate truth; however, I no longer believe this theory is completely accurate because of our power of self-deception which takes us out of the moment and disrupts the formation of a proper gestalt and allowing us to focus on internally generated factors while the truth situation is before us.

Self-deception can also keep alive a gestalt that should've dissolved back into the background while stopping the formation of a new gestalt incorporating the latest information available in the current moment. And the scariest part of self-deception is it can seriously limit what information is gathered from the environment. Self-deception tends to operate in stealth mode from the deep unconscious using fear tactics to maintain the illusion of not having contradictory internal opinions.

An example might be useful at this point. Imagine you're driving your car toward home and you realize an urgent need to find a bathroom. You envision the fastest route home and the possible impediments to your goal. The gestalt you form of this situation is a summary of all similar past experiences with their associated feelings, present experience and your projections of possible future happenings.

At this point—with a clearly defined gestalt—you can make a decision. Risk driving home or find something local. If you decide to find something local an amazing thing happens to the terrain around you. McDonald's is no longer a fast food restaurant; it transforms into a place with good parking and reasonably clean bathrooms. The Quickie Mart is similarly transformed—amazing! Businesses without accessible bathrooms don't register consciously because they're not relevant to the central need and causing them to fade into the background of our mind.

Let's assume you decide you need to go now and you see a place that you know has an accessible bathroom. Your mind flows from one gestalt to the next gestalt incorporating the relevant new information. It flows from paying attention to driving, to finding a parking spot, to parking and then to exiting the vehicle. These gestalts, with their unique sub goals, are still organized around the central need to find a bathroom.

Now let's assume you successfully accomplished to mission. The central need (find a bathroom) will no longer be the organizer of your actions. At this point something else will become central (new figure) to organizing your experience. Maybe it will be the need to wash your hands, find something to eat, or maybe you'll realize you're late and you should call home and tell someone. What becomes central next is unique to each individual and can't be predicted.

What are the key points to understand from this example?

- Meaning is generated from the elements of the gestalt.
- The central need(desire) focuses our perceptions.

If gestalt formation is a natural process for finding meaning, a wholly internal process, how can society override it? The answer lies in our physiology. A common technique is to saturate our senses with too many inputs, which leads to confusion and mental immobility. The most common technique, by far, is to short-circuit reasoning by inducing the primal need for survival. Fear (especially the fear of immediate pain) is a wonderful tool for manipulation and misdirection-if you're not living mindfully you will automatically choose to avoid pain. And because all stimuli are edited and shaped before they appear as part of a conscious gestalt, your unconscious mind can use the power of fear to limit your awareness and keep you from living in the present. I'm not a big fan of pain, any type of pain, but sometimes a little pain is necessary and appropriate. Aerobic exercise is painful for me, but it's great for my blood pressure. I'll live with the pain to get the result. I don't know whether I want to call anything "good" pain, but pain experienced with full self-awareness, that allows you to stay in the moment and avoid self-deception, is necessary pain if you want to live a meaningful life.

Our previous discussion of Gestalt formation also highlights an underappreciated aspect of our perception of the world-there is a time delay. A necessary delay because of the data limited capacity of the conscious mind and our dependence on language. We were born with the capability to form gestalts, but as we grew older we started using "prepackaged" concepts-words-which transformed the process of forming Gestalt's and find meaning.

Previous to our ability to use predefined concepts, words, we allowed the gestalt grow and evolve until meaning organically grew out of it. With the advent of language the conscious elements of a gestalt became dominate [body awareness became a secondary consideration]. And because of the limited processing capability of language based consciousness several time delays had to be inserted into the process of gestalt formation and meaning making. These time delays are ideal opportunities for diverting our attention to some internally generated event versus what is happening to us externally.

With this loss of body awareness and the domination of the conscious mind our perceptions have become overly reliant on the pre-packaged concepts (words and images) developed by our personal support systems and society at large. And this loss can lead to a rush to judgment because many of the concepts/words come to us loaded with hidden meanings and prepackaged answers from of our particular social group. These implicit assumptions can really screw with communication with people who are socialized differently, because many of the words they use, while sounding very familiar, have meanings that are entirely different from our experience. Our best hope is to minimize this impact by adopting the perspective of a baby.

What do I mean by this statement? Have you ever played the peek-a-boo game with a baby? A game where you hide your face behind your hands and the baby doesn't know where you've gone. Then you open your hands and say, "peek-a-boo." Every time you hide behind your hands the baby is mystified—where did you go? At that age babies are only aware of what it sees. They don't assume anything. What is…is!

As adults we need to do the same thing. Don't immediately assume that you understand what other people were trying to communicate and jump immediately to a judgment. Let the words define themselves within the flow of the conversation. All communications, particularly verbal communication, is prone to distortion, generalization and deletion of the facts. Therefore, always start with the surface and drill down slowly with large amounts of feedback about the accuracy of your perceptions. Philosophers would say you are adopting a phenomenological perspective.

So, what's the big deal of having a time delay between the event and your perception of it? Putting aside the philosophical question, "Does that mean we're always living in the past?" The delay between sensation and awareness opens us to the potential of becoming inauthentic. My definition of being inauthentic is when you ignore or aren't aware of your dominant need. It's really only part of my definition but, sufficient for our needs at this point. Before I return to the problem of the delay in perception, I also need to outline a simple model for the agent that is experiencing that delay in perception—the "Self". I'm going to use a simplified version of the Gestalt Therapy model of the internal structure of the Self.

In GT the Self is composed of three aspects: the I, the It and the Personality. The It is our biological body with its sensory apparatus and innate emotional capabilities; the I is our agent of action and reason; while Personality is the image that we project to ourselves and others as being responsible for what we feel or do. Given this simplified structure of the Self, let's return to the question of what happens when there's a delay involved in perception. Because there is a delay between sensing a biological need (for example, feeling thirsty.), the I aspect of the self has the opportunity to "hijack" our awareness and focus our attention on external factors and not our dominant need. Gestalt Theory would call this neurotic behavior, because the "It" is prevented by the "I" from satisfying the dominant need. Let's revisit the example of needing to find a bathroom within the context of this new information. Let's assume that you're on the way to the important business meeting and further assume that your personal identity is strongly tied to your identity as a businessman. With the delay between sensation and awareness the "I" and the "Personality" can deflect your attention from noticing places with bathrooms; leading to a painful and potentially embarrassing car ride.

Generally speaking, there are time delays embedded in every step of the natural process of awareness of a need; fulfilling that need and then stepping back and recovering from satisfying that need (GT calls this process the "cycle of experience").

Each of these delays is an opportunity to lose focus on the dominant need but, if we live with awareness and stay present with what we're trying to accomplish [right now] these delays will have minimal impact on our perception and life.

Gestalt Therapy takes it a step further and postulates that disruptions in the flow of the cycle of experience are "the" source of most psychological problems. I highly recommend Joseph Zinker's book *Creative Process in Gestalt Therapy* to get a fuller understanding of these concepts. For our purposes it sufficient to realize that by being non-judgmental, mindful, accepting of everything that's happening (that doesn't mean you necessarily agree with it; just that it is). We can avoid disrupting the cycle of experience, and stay in the moment, and avoid many psychological problems. A uninterrupted cycle of experience will minimize communication problems, greatly improve your ability to generate meaning and avoid a host of psychological problems.

This sounds like an exponential life improvement to me.

The Economics of Freedom

DO YOU HAVE an accurate picture of your present economic situation? How often do you go out to dinner? What are your fixed bills? What percentage of your monthly income goes to credit cards? At the end of the month, how much do you have left over? How stable/safe is your personal income? Your family's?

This next part is not optional! If you want to know the truth, you must do the work. Record all costs for 90 days.

QUESTION

What percentage of your income do you spend on transport, housing, utilities, entertainment, hobbies, travel, health, education, food, credit cards and savings?
Spend some time on this—this is a key task!

1.) STEP 1: Don't wait 90 days—guess.
* Record it
2.) STEP 2: Repeat it after you have collected the data for 90 days and compare. When I did it, it completely 'tripped me out!"
* Crunch the numbers using your 90 days of recorded expenses.
* Carefully record your results.

3.) STEP 3: Where were the surprises?
- Reflect and record your thoughts

Okay let's assume you have completed 90 days of documenting your income and expenditures. How much did you put in saving? Really? On your Priority List of Life where do savings rank? Pretty low, I bet. And I want to say something that I hope will change your thinking on the importance of savings. You're going to get F**KED!! Will it be your job, your health, your car, your teeth—or a wildfire? I don't know how or why, but I know it's not "if," It's when. It happens to virtually everyone and multiple times to most of us. Life happens! Good or bad, Republican or Democrat, black or white, problems are just a part of life. Think about it. It's no different from the burning out of a light bulb. It's going to happen, no matter what. You can buy high quality, high efficiency bulbs, but eventually they'll burn out (hopefully not as often as the cheap ones). Even expensive bulbs can be badly manufactured or dropped in shipping. Brownouts, lousy house wiring, power surges can kill expensive bulbs just as easily as the cheap bulbs.

So what can you do? Very little, because the truth of the matter is that over all the things that make up our lives we have very little control—even light bulbs! And that's only bad if you believe absolute control is a necessary component of a productive life. Hell, you could be dead before the next bulb burns out.

You can influence the odds but you can't control the game.

You can influence the odds but you can't control the game.

You can influence the odds but you can't control the game.

So how does this relate to the necessity of having a savings account? Let me give you an example: our car needs brakes. If you have a savings account or space on your credit cards and/or money available from your paycheck, it "ain't" no big deal. No stress, no worries. You probably won't even notice it happened. However, you should have noticed it so you can balance the use of these resources within your life plan.

Most people think that savings are for the long term—wrong! Yes, it should be a long-term consideration, but it's a really more important for short-term survival.

KEY REASONS FOR SAVINGS

1.) It gives you a buffer against the unexpected.
2.) It acts as a method for organizing the financial priorities of your life.
3.) Independence. With savings, a manageable load of monthly bills and a clear life plan you have flexibility.
4.) Long term survival, you might live to be a hundred!

To save effectively, you will need to get your financial life in order by prioritizing how you spend your money. It will also force you to adjust your lifestyle. But the hidden, mega-advantage is that you will stop substituting the spending of money to avoid building a juicy life.

QUESTIONS

How much happier would you be driving a Mercedes Benz versus a Ford? Really, how much happier?

For most of us a car is simply a tool—an expensive tool-but a tool. My personal criteria for my vehicles are simple—a tank of gas, a place for my ass and space to carry a lot of stuff. I also look at safety, low maintenance and low insurance rates. Ten years ago I downsized from a new BMW every two years to a couple of used vehicles that I will keep until they cost me too much in repairs.

The availability of a dependable vehicle gives me flexibility in where I live, where I shop and how I schedule my life. No doubt, I would miss having a car, but, man, would I enjoy sharing the expenses with a group of people (hmmmm...I need to figure out how to add this to my plan.)

Something I didn't realize until I ditched my BMW is how powerfully it had affected my self-image. I had to buy a new one every two years, or else I became worried people would think I wasn't successful. Horrors! The freaking car owned me; it was controlling how I lived my life! But eventually I realized) the only person I should worry about valuing me was...me.

Just for the sake of argument I'm going to assume you're like me, and you think you need an expensive sports car to be happy. Realistically it could be shoes, clothes, jewelry, plasma TVs or a host of other things. But for now let's assume it's an automobile. Okay, your reason for buying such an expensive vehicle is probably one of these:

- It's important to your business image.
- It's a source of personal pride and/or pleasure.
- It's necessary for your family comfort and safety.
- It's a symbol of your success or hope for success.

How's that working out for you? You should examine these reasons carefully and weigh their importance against your life goals. In my case, I must admit I rationalized my desire for jazzy sports cars with all the above reasons and more. Truth is, I didn't need any rationalizations: if I really wanted that car, and I was willing to mindfully rebalance my life space and around that choice, that would be enough. Sadly, first I decided I wanted it and then I made up my reasons afterwards. Why would I do this? Simple. I bought into the image and not the reality. I projected my life with this vehicle as being happier, safer, and more successful.

If I'd really considered the question, I would've realized the only real reason for driving a hot sports car is it's a major kick. It isn't going to make me more handsome, more successful or improve my sex life and that's okay because it shouldn't have to do any of those things. It is what it is and that's enough. So, if it doesn't compromise your life goals, enjoy! But remember that it's just a thing. I loved driving a tight mountain road with the top down on a warm California day, but that experience pales in comparison to sitting next to the people you love at the park or on a quiet walk in the mountains. Big bonus: when I'm driving it just me and the car, but on a walk, it's all about us. I know now that if I had taken the time to balance my financial situation and my time commitments, I could've done both a lot more. (sigh)

Self-Esteem, Anxiety and Depression

WHEN I BEGAN researching the concept and definition of self-esteem, I found a plethora of material that seemed to offer very contradictory information about its role. Following to my personal modus operandi, I started my readings with Gestalt psychology, which led me to Freud, which led me to Lacan. I gained some valuable insights, but I felt like I wasn't getting the whole story. After some reflection and discussions with some close friends, I really got into Alexander Lowen and Heinz Kohut. I particularly recommend *The Language of the Body and The Analysis of the Self* as excellent source material on these topics. But even after much more reading, discussion and reflection, I still felt I had an incomplete understanding of self-esteem. It was at this point I realized my beliefs about self-esteem were too narrowly defined.

My reading turned to the writings of Kierkegaard, Sartre, and other existential and postmodern philosophers. They helped. I also indulged in a number of self-help books. The light was coming on.

I then discovered the wonderful writings of R.D. Laing and Rollo May; however, I finally understood the meaning of self and self- esteem when I found Jonathan D. Brown and Nathaniel Branden. Dr. Branden's book *The Psychology of Self-Esteem* and Dr. Brown's book simply titled *The Self* led me to synthesize my investigations into a coherent view about self and self-esteem.

Before we get into the meat of this chapter, I guess I should give you my working, still evolving definition of self-esteem. It became clear after all these readings that self-esteem, a very complex concept, dependent on a multitude of internal and external processes that necessarily involve the mind, the body and society. Thankfully Dr. Branden offers a simplified definition of self-esteem in one of his books. Even though he would be the first to admit that it is incomplete, I still believe is the closest to a comprehensive definition I've seen.

> *Self-esteem is the disposition to experience oneself as competent to cope with the challenges of life and as deserving of happiness.*

This short sentence contains the essence of the meaning of self-esteem. On the surface you can see two distinct parts: the first part talks about the ability to do things (mastery) while the second part talks about value. What it doesn't talk about is how the concept of "Self" develops in parallel with the development of self-esteem. Another aspect this definition doesn't include is the ways in which social, cognitive, interpersonal and emotional processes combine to create this effect. He couldn't include it in a general definition because it's different for each person. Each person's sense of self-esteem will contain both elements, but their proportions are unique for each person.

Why do I bundle together the processes of anxiety, depression and self-esteem? I believe they are inseparable. It's tough to have high self-esteem while suffering from anxiety or depression. And I seriously doubt you will experience severe anxiety or depression if your self-esteem is good. So, in reality, to modify any one of these, you have to modify all of them. Let's start by discussing a key aspect of self-esteem.

How much time each day do you spend making love? Not having sex, but making love? Making love can be completely separate from having sex, and I'm a big fan of both. On average, how often do you express feelings of love? I know what you're going to say. You're not married, involved or have a significant relationship at this time.

WRONG!

Look in the mirror. The reflection you see is now and forever your most significant relationship. So make sure every day you spread some love on yourself. My recommendation is to layer it on thick. And don't forget about Fido or Lassie or Mr. Chuckles and remember to throw in a few positives for your house plants, too. And, you can't go wrong calling your mother, brother, sister or uncle and expressing some deep feelings to these trusted loved ones. Part of my work in my process group with depressed people is to get them to crawl outside themselves. Just making this effort to express warmth to other human beings seems to help. Don't be shy about it, and let it out. Make it real, and make it from the heart because love does make the world go round. Corny but true. If you let a day go by without making love, you've wasted a day.

I can't stress enough the importance of self-love. Self-love isn't about ignoring your faults or enhancing an already enlarged ego. It's about loving the person you are right now! Yes, you need to change this or that about yourself and that will always be true. Needing to change isn't a fault. It's a necessity if you want to continue growing in this life. So drop the judgment and allow yourself to change and grow as the situation demands. The day you totally accept and love all of you-the good, the bad and the ugly—is the day you will have total victory. I'm completely serious. The first law of cybernetics teaches us that "the component of a system that has the most flexibility controls the system." You might want to meditate on that idea.

If you can completely and totally love and accept yourself as you are now, you're automatically positioned to make some serious changes. Not because of society or because of some idealized image you aspire to emulate or because your mother told you to, but because you want to improve your life and the lives of the people around you.

Why is it only possible to make big changes if you start from the position of self-acceptance? With self-acceptance you are no longer vested in any of your behaviors or habits. Acceptance is not resignation. Acceptance allows awareness that puts you in contact with who you are right now and is the first step to change.

Whether these habits are good or bad, you can change them! Gestalt Therapy theory says you can only change by being and accepting the person you really are right now rather than by acting like the person you think you want to become. With total love and acceptance, the parts of yourself that have lain hidden in your unconscious can now express themselves openly. No longer will they need to subtly influence your perception of the world so that they can continue to operate unnoticed. Now change can happen. It will be a fight, but a fight you can/will win.

By the way, I wasn't just talking about your negative characteristics. Both negative and positive—habitual perceptual stances—limit awareness of what is truly happening at this moment. Generally speaking, we don't worry about the positive habits, but we should. They can be just as limiting as any negative perceptual habit when you need to adapt creatively to a new situation and you're unaware of their influence.

Committing yourself to living with total self-acceptance means accepting your primal instincts, too. That's something most people prefer not to discuss. Primal instincts are not socially acceptable, so if you act on them, you can turn yourself into a social outcast or worse. Mindlessly repressing these desires will significantly influence your perception of the world,, a classic Catch-22. Nietzsche recognizes this problem and clearly believes that these instincts are part of the true nature of humankind He also believes the socially dictated repression of these instincts is the basis of what we can call the soul; most significantly he believes that their repression effectively stops man from evolving into Superman, the "ubermensch."

I'm a great fan of Nietzsche. He is one of history's greatest observers of civilized man and he is an excellent logician. However, I'm sure in this case that he really got it wrong. Considering all possible explanations, I seriously doubt that the soul is composed of repressed instinctual drives – But, who knows for certain? A more probable reason for the repression of primal instincts lies in the formation of civilization. Within social groups DNA propagates more successfully when anti-social instincts are repressed. I'm sure you can see the transformation from "lone wolf" to pack member would require some big changes. Truth is, living in any social group requires the sacrifice of some individual freedoms—and instinctual drives—to receive the benefits of that group. It's called the social contract. It's a good trade, but we must stay aware of repressions, or, at the worst times, these "dark" energies will surface to bite us in the…posterior and sabotage our feelings of self-love and acceptance.

Modern neurology has clued us into another weird aspect of being human. You can love yourself completely and totally and still completely hate yourself. From love to hate back to love in a flash! Mix a dash of bad luck with a little disappointment and we can fall into subconscious depression and self-loathing while consciously believing everything is going okay. It's it happens all the time, but most people somehow manage not to notice it! Then, they can't understand why they're having problems sleeping or why they have such a lack of energy or why they have this sense of foreboding. Their body is trying to tell them, but social conditioning and a lack of body awareness are not allowing the message to get through to the conscious mind.

The secret is to pay attention to this body-based 911 and deal with it now! The necessary first step is to become consciously aware of that there is a problem. The real advantage of "living in the now" with a phenomenological perspective is that you have integrated your mind and body and minimized the possibility of a subconscious disconnect. Using the tools of mindfulness and meditation, you can bring any nagging feelings easily to the surface. I have to inject an important warning at this point. Don't buy into the idea that you must be happy and joyful all the time even though most of society will tell you that's the way it's supposed to be-it ain't going to happen. Second, don't try to avoid the darkness because there is much to learn there-just don't let it set up long-term housekeeping. I'm not saying search out your dark side (it will find you all by itself), but acknowledge it and understand its truth. Depression, self-loathing and darkness serve an important short-term purpose in making you aware of problems. If you're generally a pretty emotionally balanced person, there's probably an important message there in the dark that can improve your life.

Be smart about it. You don't go to the hospital for a scraped knee, but you certainly should go for a broken leg. If your depression is deep and sustained, bring in the professionals. Get help! For the everyday "the- world- sucks"—but- I-don't-want-to-kill myself—or—others kind of depression, be open to experiencing these emotions and understanding their messages. The work can be painful and embarrassing (and I'm sure it's not something you want to expose in front of others), but do it anyway. The French have a saying, "Joy shared is doubled, misery shared is halved." Find someone you can trust. It doesn't matter if it's a process group, a counselor/therapist, a rabbi/priest/shaman or a close friend. My choice is the Gestalt therapy hot seat. It works for me. Find what works for you.

KEY POINTS ABOUT DEPRESSION AND ANXIETY

* Much of life is choice but anxiety, depression and blackness happens without conscious input. Don't judge. Accept.

- Don't automatically try to fix the problem! Honor it. Be present with it and feel it! Open yourself to its energy, relax and follow.
- When depressed, focus on key beliefs and values. Be clear on what your most important goal is right now and use it to keep yourself focused and moving forward.
- Pay attention to what you love.
- Get some exercise.
- Laugh a lot!
- Don't allow yourself to overindulge in anything including exercise or laughter.

When you're depressed or suffering chronic anxiety, your energy and your focus goes out the window. Passion is forgotten and negative emotions flow through your consciousness with tsunami-like force.

Let your emotions flow without judgment.

I can't stress the following enough. Breath, relax and don't run away from them, but don't hold on to them either. A common problem I have observed with the mild to moderately depressed is their inability to decide anything. You take them out to lunch, and they can't decide what they want from the menu. Nothing looks interesting. If, perchance, you find yourself in a similar situation, I recommend your finding some of their favorite places to go for lunch and what their favorite things are to eat and decide for them.

We all want to be independent, but don't let your pride stop you from helping a friend when they need it. Consider the flipside of this arrangement when you are depressed. Allow others to help you. Allow them to take you to lunch. Allow them to help you order if you're stymied. I realize that you're probably less fun than a funeral when you're depressed, but your friends and family can handle that. Let them. Depression gets stronger when you isolate yourself. Depression is the time to join the herd. Don't allow yourself to hang out on the periphery even if that's your normal place. Join the pack.

Let me give you an example.

After finishing my doctoral studies at Penn State, I joined a startup company in Rolling Meadows, Illinois. It was a supercharged, high stress, technical wonderland and I loved it. I ate it, dreamed it, and lived it to the hilt. And when the company failed, a wave of depression hit me like a ten-ton hammer. I literally had to been told to eat and go to bed. I sat on the couch for hours without even bothering to turn on the television. I was numb!

My wife, a very smart woman, let me sit there for a while, but then she started to take me to the park in the afternoon and then for a walk in the evening. It helped, but I still couldn't face the idea of taking another high-tech job at that point. She suggested I start working temp jobs. Some of them didn't turn out very well, but then I got a job setting up equipment and doing security for rock concerts. I spent many hours on my feet and got low pay—not to mention a waste of the ten years I had spent in college. But that job was the right one for that time. Slowly at first, I found my energy returning. Frequently I returned home late at night with more energy than when I had left. My wife noticed it first. As I look back on it now, it's pretty obvious. I was still pretty depressed, but when I returned home at 2 A.M. and tried to interest my wife in sex, something was changing. I found I was feeding off the giant cauldron of energy that is a rock concert.

I started looking forward to going to work. I started to read again. At first it was pulp fiction. Later I found myself at the engineering library reading the journals. I still wasn't "my old self," but I was starting to do the things that made me happy. At this point I returned to the gym and started working out fanatically. I became obsessed with getting in shape. I developed delusions of becoming a great tri-athlete. I still have a problem with the injuries that I caused myself during this period. Luckily I didn't do any serious damage—permanent, yes, serious, no. Eventually, overtraining led to an injury that required me to cut back on my training. That in itself led to another bout of depression, perhaps not as deep but still incapacitating. The cycles of manic highs and black lows became shorter and shorter, and over time and I was able to continue working security and reading journals. Then one day about six months into this journey I announced to my wife, "I think it's time to go back to work." And I did. The bouts of depression and manic highs and lows still happened but with less severity and frequency. They still happen, but now I have ways to handle them.

During that period of my life I refused to go to a doctor or visit a counselor. I could have saved myself a great deal of suffering if I could have been persuaded to visit a psychiatrist and/or pop a few pills. And if I had done the work I suggest in this book, I could've avoided most of those manic ups and downs. Sigh. Perhaps I wouldn't be the person I am today if I'd avoided that. Perhaps I would have become an even better person. After you've been bitten by a poisonous snake, you find it's hard to be nice to harmless ones. Once bitten, twice shy.

The "upside" to this roller-coaster period in my life was it awakened my curiosity about how to live a "juicy" life. So, I took more psychology courses, explored various spiritual paths and eventually discovered Gestalt Therapy. The Gestalt methodology really turned me on my head. I had always been a man who prided himself in living a life of the mind—and the body be damned.

Gestalt awakened me to the obvious truth that if the body dies, so does the mind. By integrating the mind and body we maximize our ability to really enjoy life. But the most important lesson this experience taught me was to live authentically. It also provided me with a toolset and a methodology to succeed. GT also trained me in putting my talents to work while encouraging me to apply my genius to my life (thank you, Oscar Wilde). The key GT tools are sprinkled throughout the book and in Appendix

Woody Smith

A, which includes a short list of my favorite GT books.

How specifically does GT help with avoiding or handling depression?

Fritz Perls (developer of GT) uses the analogy of eating to describe the process of handling and processing inputs. Fritz explains that we should always eat mindfully. That we should be mindfully aware of every bite we put in our mouth and completely chew and digest it before we take another bite. He believes that this process applies equally to our emotions. Fritz believes that we can healthfully digest complex and often contradictory emotional material the same way we digest a good steak and glass of wine—one swallow at a time.

Let's walk through the process. Imagine cutting off a reasonable size bite of steak/fish/tofu. Now, with mindful awareness, lift this tempting morsel to your mouth. Observe it as you lift it toward your mouth, enjoy the enticing aroma and notice the sensations you experience as it settles on your tongue. Stays engaged with this bite of steak and chew it completely. Notice how the flavor and aroma evolves as you continue to chew this delectable morsel. What sensations does your mouth feel? Now, swallow. What feelings does it evoke in the body? What other sensations are you aware of as you swallow this morsel? Now take a moment to complete the experience. Breathe and relax for just a moment and let the experience complete itself fully. Now, you may want a sip of wine or another bite of steak or a forkful of salad. It's your choice. Nobody's controlling you. You have complete freedom over your next action. Don't gloss over it. Be there with it.

Are you seeing the parallel between the process of eating and the process of digesting new information? Fritz believes that eating is the basic, fundamental process of living. He believes we develop all our decision-making capabilities from this basic decision process of "I like this or I don't like this." He firmly believes that all the processes we develop as we grow-up are just refinements

39

of this original process.

What does this mean to us in relation to depression? Here are my insights and formula:

- Watch what you're doing with your food and you will understand how you handle your emotions
- Carefully and mindfully watch for disruptions in "cycle of the experience" (COE) to see where depression is derailing your life.

The COE consists of 4 basic steps (break it down to finer increments if you like):

Step one: Be aware of any desires calling you.
Step two: Engage mindfully with these desires.
Step three: Act or don't act
Step four: Complete the experience-and let it go and return to a balanced awareness pregnant with fresh choices.

It's at this point (step 2) when I talk of fully engaging this desire, that phenomenological perspective comes in. If you want this formula to succeed, you must withhold judgment until you reach step three. Notice how this process is circular and flows from body to mind and back again. Neither body nor mind is given preference. They are co-equals in this continuous cycle of desire, awareness, action/judgment, and completion, followed by a return to the beginning. The completion of the previous cycle releases and increases that vested energy to use in the next cycle. Fritz believes that when this "cycle of experience" is working, your life will be working. It doesn't mean that everything will go smoothly, but it does mean you'll have a method to work through the bumps in the road.

I have found this particular process invaluable when working with negative emotions and anxiety. When you completely digest a negative emotion using this process, it no longer exists separately within your being. And when it's no longer separate, compartmentalized, hidden in your subconscious, it's possible to handle it. Remember, negative emotions exist because they had a real survival advantages at some point in our evolutionary history. So-called negative emotions like fear and anxiety can save your life. Don't let society and its feel-good message make you ignore the importance of such negative feelings. Fear is present-centered and survival-oriented. It only becomes negative when your fear becomes chronic. It's only when fear of fear starts controlling your life that it becomes a problem. Feelings of anxiety are usually future based and can serve you well if they help you focus on significant future-based problems.

The big problem with fear and anxiety is that they tend to take us out of the moment and disrupt the natural flow (cycle) of experience. Add an extra dash of anxiety or a smidgen more of fear, and we can find ourselves spinning off into the dark side. With minimal prodding we allow ourselves to lose focus of what's real and alive in the moment and turn inward to memory, fantasy and projection. Before civilization and socialization co-opted fear and anxiety for its own purposes, we would have quickly evaluated the sources of these new tensions and resolved them and gotten on with life. In our present world most of us tend either to ignore them or to obsess over them. Neither is a good idea. How did we let these useful, body-based skills get perverted?

Sadly, we tend to absorb negative beliefs and values about ourselves from our social-economic system , which grossly exaggerates these emotions and contributes to making them chronic. We have been socialized to uncritically and mindlessly absorb many of these judgments without digesting them. These freshly minted, undigested judgments take up residence in our unconscious and become hidden values and beliefs that shape our perceptions and dictate what information we pay attention to about our self and others.

Warning! Warning! Warning!

In a healthy lifestyle you must let your thoughts flow in their natural cycles of negative and positive intent with acceptance while avoiding pre-judgment until you have mindfully digested the content. I hope you noticed I said "healthy lifestyle." Are you living a healthy lifestyle?

If you're not living a healthy lifestyle, nothing will work.
If you're not living a healthy lifestyle, nothing will work.
If you're not living a healthy lifestyle, nothing will work.

Besides a couple of my favorite philosophers, I also had a professor who believed that you should always say important things three times. He believed that you might not understand what he was saying at that moment, but at some time in the future you would be capable of understanding, and he wanted to make damn sure you remembered what he said.

It's time to get out your journal and write down what you understand about your present lifestyle.

KEY QUESTIONS

- Is your present career congruent with your values and beliefs?
- Who do you hang out with?
- What new things are you learning?
- How much time do you spend thinking, reflecting or just chilling out?
- Have you done any long-range planning lately?
- Does all your news come from TV?
- How much sleep are you getting? (New parents can skip this one.)
- Do you take regular vacations?
- How much time do you spend making love—not

necessarily involving sex?

- Do you have a complete social network of friends, family and neighbors? Do you communicate with them regularly?
- Do you have any money in your pocket at the end of the month?
- Are you making progress on your life goals?
- How's your self-esteem?
- Are you reaching outside yourself to help others?
- Do you have time to exercise?
- How much time do you get to do nothing?
- What's your big dream?
- When's the last time you took yourself out on a date?
- When's the last time you told somebody you love him/her?
- When's the last time you told yourself that you love yourself?
- How about those Mets?
- When's the last time you visited a dentist?
- How's your blood pressure?

Now, make up 20 more questions and answer them!

Write them all down. Mull them over. Kick the cat (metaphorically speaking) if you need to. Digest them fully. How do they fit with your previous planning?

I know I'm making you repeat part of the planning exercise from an earlier chapter, but this time it's from a different angle. Hopefully, if you did the previous strategic planning session, you're a different person now.

Understandably, many people exhibit major anxiety when we talk about lifestyle changes. As I said before, anxiety focuses on the future, and lifestyle changes removes the illusion of continuity. Realistically, no one can guarantee that the future will be like the past, but memory and imagination allow us to project our future as if it could be the same or better without changing anything. Fat chance! You can see I'm pretty emphatic about developing a healthy lifestyle because I've seen the results. What do I consider a healthy lifestyle? It varies widely from person to person, but this book can help you define the proper mix that works for you.

This chapter is titled *Self-Esteem, Anxiety and Depression*, so why the discussion on lifestyle? Well, I've seen the powerful effect that lifestyle has on these three factors. I'm not talking about being gay or straight or Democrat or Republican or tall or short, black or white when I say "lifestyle." I'm asking whether your life is going to be a positive or negative net gain for the world.

A healthy lifestyle makes the three horsemen of gloom tend much more manageable. But even in a healthy lifestyle, up-down cycles exist. And, when self-esteem cycles down and anxiety and depression cycle, up what's the cure?

ACCEPTANCE! ACCEPTANCE! ACCEPTANCE!

You must accept the good and bad with equal balance. Refuse to identify with either because neither is you. Life is a constant swirl of chance and choice, and the only thing you can really control is yourself. The degree of control you can assert is highly dependent on a healthy lifestyle.

The keys to controlling your life are:

- Knowing who you are
- Knowing where you are going
- Knowing what you believe
- Being mindfully involved in the direction of your life.

You're never going to have complete control, but by exerting your Will while maintaining a mindful, perspective, you will be in the best possible position to control what you can and to accept the outcome of what you can't.

While American society may celebrate individuality, it negates it as well by producing a population of conformist consumers. After all, it's much easier to sell to a flock of sheep than it is to lone wolves. Remember what I said previously? The sovereign purpose of society is to propagate our DNA. Society forces everyone to conform to the norm in order to maximize such propagation.

Why?

Because "normal" people tend to minimize risk and maximize survival. This may be great for the propagation of DNA, but it's not so great for the advancement of society or for us as consumers. And once you understand this societal motivation for normalization, you can also understand why society favors the positive emotions-they're more predictable and safer. The upside to obeying society's rules and norms is that, statistically speaking, you have a better chance of surviving—but at the very high price of self knowledge.

Here's the problem: how do we play the social game and still grow and evolve personally?

A final note about the use of "fear" in a consumer society.

Fear is undoubtedly the #1 technique used to sell most everything in our society. Sometimes the government or your mother or your best friend is trying to sell you something good and sometimes they are just trying to sell you something. And it's going to work if you don't stay mindfully aware and process/digest their influences before you allow them to take up residence.

This is far from an exhaustive treatment of these topics. I would dare say it's pretty superficial, but I'm following the 80/20 Principle. Often called the Pareto principle, it states that you get 80% of your results from 20% of your effort. I'm trying to help you identify that 20%. I know I'm pretty close because I've tried out this material on a large number of people in my process group over the years and they've found it useful.

From discussions in group it's clear that many of them added additional ingredients and modified the recipe. Then they baked it to suit their own tastes. This is what I hope you do, too.

Warning: Expectations Ahead

THIS CHAPTER IS about learning to separate expectations from goals. Goals can be a very loaded word. The word "goal" should denote a decision to spend time and effort in completing a task or reach a predefined outcome. Unfortunately, we often forget that a goal is just one step in a much larger process. We become fixated on achieving these goals without looking at their relevance to the bigger picture of living. Additionally, we frequently tie grandiose expectations to the attainment of these goals. You know the ones! My mother will love me if I graduate first in my class. If I make this much money, then I'll be a success. When the kids grow up, I'll have time to do my own thing. Every one of them a fantasy!

We've become lost in the world of cause and effect. Our neocortex has given us this wonderful ability to dream, make inferences, and generalize. Used in combination with memory, it gives us the illusion we can predict the future. And happily for us, it tends to work out that way. My car starts 999 times out of a 1000. So, I come to expect it to start every time, but when it doesn't (damn, left the lights on again), I may become angry and disappointed. I've built this expectation on past history that every time I try to start the car it will start, but not for any logical reason. I just expect it to.

Usually when I get into my vehicle I have a destination in

mind [i.e. a goal] and if I'm not careful, I also have an unconscious expectation and reward coupled with it. There is the rub.

Somehow we've managed to turn a high probability outcome to a certainty. My belief is we've turned the useful scientific principle of cause and effect into an over-generalized Universal truth. We now assume that the same or similar events will produce the same result as was previously exhibited. We've forgotten about the possibility of multiple outcomes from the same cause or that the results are time-dependent (Is that why we always try to fight the next war like we fought the last one?).

I've found cats and kids to be my greatest teachers on the fallibility of cause and effect. With cats and kids be prepared to have any and all expectations mutilated, violated and transformed. Adults are more predictable because of socialization, while kids and cats are who they are and not who I and society think they should be. With my cats I have minimal expectations and high acceptance for who they are. With my children I wish I could say that was also true.

As I've grown older, my acceptance of their uniqueness has also grown, but only been in the last handful of years have I learned to separate goals from expectations. As a parent you always will have goals that you hope your children will achieve because you believe if they will then have the best chance of leading a fulfilling life.

The problem sets in that you tie your expectations of a fulfilling life to a specific outcome in their unique process of living. In this case expectations can be a real bitch. The central problem is cats and kids are their own beings. They have their own internal lives and their own reasons for doing things. We may be able to influence them and hopefully make them aware of the external influences trying to control them, but we can't control their decision-making processes. Of course, this begs the question, why have expectations?

The correct answer is that you shouldn't.

I have many good reasons for not having expectations but not one good reason for having them. This is not to say you shouldn't plan. I think you should plan for every reasonable outcome you can anticipate, but you should not be emotionally tied to any particular outcome. If your preferred outcome happens, enjoy the moment, but if your preferred outcome doesn't happen, you can still enjoy yourself. Life is about the journey, not the destination.

As I mentioned previously, expectations make you dependent on the fantasy of cause and effect. You also become emotionally invested in one particular outcome. Thirdly, you waste energy. If you can't control the outcome-only influence it at best-what good is it to invest yourself in a particular outcome?

Reason four for avoiding expectations is a doozy: all expectations come with a fixed perspective. Think how limiting that is to someone trying to live a brilliant life. No longer do you see your cats and kids as the beings they are in this moment. Your viewpoint of them will be forever fixed at the time of the birth of your expectations for them. From that moment on you will view them through the perspective of those expectations. All their accomplishments, changes and transformations will be viewed in reference to these unfulfilled, future-based expectations. You'll end up missing a lot of joy and happiness if you get trapped living for the future and not celebrating in the present.

This great quotation from John F. Kennedy illustrates my next reason:

> *Some men die in war and others are badly wounded.*
> *While other men never leave the country. Life isn't fair.*

JFK wasn't bitter even though he had lost a brother and was badly wounded himself. He simply understood that life doesn't guarantee anyone anything, so you should find as much joy as possible and expect nothing in return. He's not saying you shouldn't treat people fairly, but he is saying not to expect them to treat you fairly in return. You can't know and will never know what factors- external and internal- are motivating others at this particular moment. Don't try. Kennedy is also saying, "Live now!" because you don't know what tomorrow will bring.

My sixth reason for avoiding expectations is that they don't lead to a healthy lifestyle. Expectations are future based and require that you define and fix your personality and goals around these expectations, removing yourself from living in the present - ouch! Additionally, you're now measuring yourself against a phantasm over which you have no control. How can this be healthy?

My final reason for avoiding expectations involves personal belief systems. Sometimes you don't live up to your beliefs. Typically the psychological pain you feel will tempt you to fabricate excuses and isolate (repress) the "part" of yourself that failed. Some psychologists say that failure to meet this type of expectation induces you to splinter yourself psychically and emotionally and repress these offending emotions to avoid damaging your self image. Think how harmful this can be in the long run. Every expectation that's not met further limits your perceptions and emotional responses to the world around you.

The question is what can you do about it?

- The most important thing to avoid is becoming attached to your goals
- Be flexible.
- Always have a plan B.
- Always keep the big picture in mind.
- How does your goal fit with your overall life plan?
- Accept both good and bad outcomes with the same attitude.
- Don't let society define the value of this goal.
- You are not your goals.
- Stay present and aware.

- On the bigger goals spend some time thinking, reflecting, praying or meditating before you commit to them.
- When a goal has an expectation attached to it understand it. Did you generate it or was it some external factor?
- What does the expectation say about this goal?
- Is this expectation congruent with my beliefs?
- Why didn't you notice that this goal had an expectation attached to it?

MEGA HINT

Don't tie your Self-Esteem to your goals.

MEGA HINT

Don't tie your Self-Esteem to your goals

MEGA HINT

Don't tie your Self-Esteem to your goals.

You will never completely de-couple goals and expectations, but kept trying! Also be aware that many goals and expectations can be completely subconscious if you are not living with self-awareness. These situations, when you are not self-aware, are the breeding grounds for self-deception. Consciously you may have zero expectations, but subconsciously you may be driving an eighteen-wheeler full of them.

Self-Deception

I ATTEMPTED TO introduce all the topics in previous chapters as separately as possible, while noting their obvious overlaps and interconnectedness. But this topic-self-deception- requires us to use them as an integrated whole. An interesting problem is that many of our beliefs and values change with the situation. Problems that appear similar but occur in different social situations can evoke different emotions, moods, and I believe this is the principal cause of self-deception.

Self-deception is a negative aspect of a very positive ability— multi-perspective thinking. If we don't control this ability, we end up ingesting opinions as truth without being consciously aware of what we've done, which leaves us wide open to the possibility of self-deception. I'm sure you have had the experience of a trusted love one's telling you something and your acting on that information immediately without thinking, but even as you act , you're "gut" is asking, "what's going on here?" It happened to me regularly until the "cycle of experience" and mindfulness became my standard ways of operating in the world.

Our evolutionary development has given us a wonderful tool—consciousness. But consciousness is just the newest layer to an already complex bio-computer. We were already equipped with a fine computational instrument that we now call the hippocampus/amalyga. It's a wickedly fine network for doing real time survival calculations—among other things. But what this gland lacks is the ability to imagine, to dream, and to work with abstractions. In contrast, the recently evolved neo-cortex empowers us to do all these things and even more importantly, it gives us an awareness of BEING. We are self-aware. But, before we go all existential, consider the survival advantage consciousness gives us. As a species we aren't very strong, fast, well armored or camouflaged; we needed an advantage if we were going to survive. Did consciousness arise because of divine intervention, random evolution or a lucky mutation? Who cares!

The perplexing aspect about consciousness for me is its dominance. Let's reflect for a moment on what's important in life. With me, all the really important things in life are old brain/body things, such as love, friendship, compassion, fear and anger. Thank the goddess for consciousness because it makes abstract thought possible (and I can't imagine living without it), but we also need to realize that conscious thought is a very small part of the whole game. Why, then, does modern civilization so prize Apollonian consciousness and devalue Dionysian irrationality?

The word rational is from the Latin and originally also meant "to weigh." Today, we usually define rational to mean logical reasoning. Finite, binary logic is an externally learned attribute and is, therefore, public. On the other hand, irrational Dionysian "reasoning" isn't so clear cut. Dionysian reasoning rejects dualism (black or white only, no gray), accepts paradox and embraces the subjective. Putting it another way, rational thinking is based on external knowledge while irrational thinking is internal, private and mostly subconscious. Example: I lived on a commune while I was in graduate school. One day Rhianna decided she needed to paint her new steamer trunk the house colors. We didn't have a garage and Greg was cutting the grass in the back yard and the other residents were weeding the gardens. So, she decided to paint the trunk in the front yard...naked. This made a lot of sense to us because paint tends to get on everything and it's easier to take a shower than to get paint off of a pair of blue jeans. Of course, we never thought that the new minister and his wife would show up to introduce themselves and save a few pagan souls. So by trusting in the infinite wisdom of Dionysus, we got a double bonus. Bonus one, getting to watch a naked, busty, redhead, paint and frolic on a warm summer's day. Bonus two, scaring off a Baptist minister on a mission. Hail Dionysus! Hidden bonus three, we didn't have to buy a new pair of jeans.

Can you see the contradictory perspectives involved here? Logically within the context of our parents' world, we screwed up big time. In our world it made perfect sense. Both views are completely correct within their separate social ecosystems. Embrace the rules of your own social "ecosystem," but when dealing with those outside it, your best hope is to adopt a non-judgmental, zero-expectation perspective, let situations evolve naturally, and adapt.

What happens if the other group doesn't know what it believes? Prepare for a long period of education. Hopefully, with time and will a bridge can be built, but be prepared for some big negatives if the separate groups are competing for the same limited resources. Now, can you see why society wants everyone to believe the same thing? After all, survival decreases with conflict. It is in society's best interest that we absorb these beliefs without conscious thought—no personal power allowed! If you are consciously aware of your beliefs, you can change them, and society may not approve. My friend Steve adds if you are aware of society's rules, you can avoid being controlled by them. He also taught me something else about awareness with a simple question.

If you don't know the reasons for your moral beliefs, are you truly a moral person are just one that hasn't been tested yet?

Ouch!

By this time, I hope you're seeing and feeling the wide implications of self-deception. It's one of society's most effective tools for social control. Even though social control is necessary even in a democracy it should be a conscious process and not a tool for manipulation. A single child and a civilization both need clearly defined boundaries to maximize growth; however, without mindful awareness every boundary and rule will eventually degenerate into mindless dogma.

Can you see the bigger problem? In our modern society we have absorbed many of our beliefs without conscious awareness. And many of these beliefs contradict one other. Beliefs may have been useful in their right contexts, but what about right now in this moment? Which belief should be activated in this new situation? Logic in this case will get us nowhere because we aren't consciously aware of the criteria we use to make decisions. And if the social situation demands a decision right now, what can we do? Previously, when I was unaware of my beliefs I would turn to my support network—society—for direction. This is a lot like playing poker with your cards turned facing your opponents. They know what you are holding and you don't have a clue what they're holding. Not a fair deal, but that's how society likes to play the game.

There's another even more subtle problem with this process. Frequently when faced with these logically impossible situations, our decision is not to decide. In many cases this is a good idea, but by doing so we have generated an internal, conscious and subconscious paradox. If we're to remove this paradox from our conscious mind, we will have to repress it and that requires using up mental resources to continue to repress it until we solve it somehow. This isn't going to happen because we don't have the information we need to solve it. Over time we accumulate a vast amount of "unfinished business" which requires us to consume mental resources just to maintain the status quo.

I've found the key to avoiding self-deception is making sure that you fully "digest" your mental meal and fully break it down to its component parts before you absorb and integrate them. It's crucial that your mind and body agree. By integrating your logical, Apollonian consciousness with your emotive, Dionysian subconscious, you don't waste your mental resources; instead, you can use all that energy to make positive changes. But, if you can't reconcile your mind and body, you better have a darn good reason for siding with one over the other.

KEY POINT

Don't always default to your conscious mind.
Dionysian, body-based reasoning is as important as
logical reasoning. Don't privilege either!

Here's an example: if you see a friend fall on their ass at church in front of 200 acquaintances and your friend ask, "Did I look really stupid and did everybody notice?"

What would you answer? Logically the correct answer is yes and nearly everyone.

From the Dionysian perspective the correct answer is, "absolutely not and hardly anyone noticed."

The first response may appear to be "factually" more truthful, but I believe on balance the second response is the more correct and truthful- for the totality of the person in that moment. Later, I suspect that the integration of mind and emotion will led to great laughter and a really funny story to tell at family gatherings.

Woody Smith

Will and Intention

YOU WILL NEVER accomplish what you desire without the power of will and intention. The first he first step in developing a Will of Iron requires you to become mindfully aware of your goals and needs versus those society imposes on you. Authentic goals and needs flow naturally from your own, unique overall plan.

However, life is dynamic and new situations often require new goals, but these new goals should still be completely congruent with your beliefs. Don't short-circuit the goal development process! Spend the time needed to mindfully understand the consequences of your beliefs and goals.

Reflect. Meditate. Pray.

Try to understand how your beliefs create your goals and see how they affect your overall vision and life direction. Then, with this new understanding, invoke the power of Intention.

Intention, I believe, is a mix of spirituality, politics, consciousness and emotional investment. Intention is the focusing tool that, when used correctly, optimally aligns you with the forces that swirl around you. Happily, Quantum theory has shown us that an active observer can affect the outcome of even the most elementary interactions. In truth, quantum mechanical experiments usually consist of a few controllable and observable variables; unfortunately, life has an unlimited number of nonlinear, interacting variables that are not necessarily controllable or observable. Always remember the world we live in is a complex system of nonlinear, constantly interacting processes that create a web of visible and invisible forces. But the effect of the observer appears to hold even in the most complex systems. Mindful Intention is the tool that can help you get to the heart of these complex situations. The power of Intention lies in its independence from exclusively conscious thinking.

Let's talk about the two spiritual dimensions of intention. Dimension one requires getting in touch with your "higher" self, (Eileen) which, by allowing you to get that aerial perspective, removes you from the sway of social forces. Dimension two consists of spirit energy, an invisible engine that will help you broadcast your goals across the many dimensions of your life. Chaos theory shows us that everything in life is connected. I tend to imagine it as an infinite network of connected pipes. When I was young, my brother's bedroom was on the third floor and mine was on the first. We used to send messages back and forth to each other by banging on the heating pipes. The web of networks that we call life is obviously much more complex and only partially visible, so my advice is to pray, meditate, reflect and ritualize constantly whenever starting or continuing any important task.

The power of Intention is about aligning yourself mentally, physically and spiritually in ways that best serve you in reaching your goals.

Intentionality also has serious political overtones. By definition politics is about power and control. Modern society has mechanisms devoted exclusively to determining who gets how much of what and when by rewarding those who follow the rules and penalizing those who don't. From the standpoint of society, acting on personal intentions rather than on societal ones is a subversive act [breaking the law, breaking the law...]. Luckily for us, former Speaker of the House Tip O'Neill taught us the secret to all political power: "All politics are local." He showed us that, even though our political world is one giant system, true power and control flows from a local base. The power of intentionality can sometimes bypass this system and go directly to the source, but usually it has to work through our normal channels. So, what can you do? Answer: use the power of intention to influence the people who think they have control and power—because sometimes they do. Always spend some of your time building your networks because the more possible paths you have to your destination, the more likely you are to get there.

KEY POINT

*Use your journal to record interesting and useful
additions to your personal and professional networks.*

My brother and I lived in a three-story, prairie style farmhouse with heating pipes running in a continuous network from the basement to the third floor. What would have happened if we had lived in separate "wings" in a one-story ranch home instead?

I've already talked about the role of conscious awareness and emotion in relation to the power of intention, but I feel I need to say a few more words. I've seen that the power of intention influences all the modes of existence, and I know from personal experience this influence is not always positive. Sometimes focus becomes a set of blinders, limiting perception and potential emotional range. Living with awareness allows us to creatively adapt as new opportunities present themselves and to consciously avoid becoming emotionally attached to one particular outcome. Using the power of intention effectively necessitates living with awareness and without pre-judgment or expectations.

KEY POINT

Record your observations.

Remember, society has its own goals and it doesn't really care about you until your goals collide with its goals. Society will act toward you with passive indifference so long as your goals are congruent or with active interference if you differ; either way, society is always trying to entangle you in its plans. This is not necessarily bad, but it is a complication that you should be mindfully aware of.

Now let's talk about Will. Will is a primal force that screams to you "Live!" when it may be easier just to give up. It is also the force that helps you keep moving in the direction of your goals after you have clarified your intentions. It's important to start any significant task by sorting out your personal desires from society's desires for you.

Intention and Will mutually support each other and help carry you toward your goals. The real importance of will power comes to the fore when you face a problem that requires a new solution or one that places you in direct conflict with your "ecosystem." Both of these situations can put you into the court of public pressure, where the primary tool of manipulation and control is premature judgment—judgments using society's beliefs and goals.

These situations require our full toolbox of techniques:

- Mindfulness to make us aware.
- A phenomenological perspective to prevent previous experience from biasing us.
- A lack of expectations to allow us to experiment with new solutions, and high self-esteem that is completely independent of this goal.

Even with these tools, we can expect emotional hits because we will inevitably come into more conflict with our ecosystem as we grow personally. Be prepared for highs and lows if the goal is contrary to the interests of your ecosystem. The peaks are easy, but what do you need to survive these valleys?

The key to overriding the negative emotions and sense of diminishing self-esteem that occurs during these situations is Will power. Will power, coupled with the TOTE process and the rest of the tools, can help you find the solution you need. The most important skill for solving problems and reaching goals is the ability to go from one failure to the next failure to the next without diminishing your enthusiasm for finding a solution. Will power is your shield to keep moving forward when the answer isn't coming and the agents of social pressure are telling you to move on or conform to the status quo.

Another important aspect of will power is knowing when to quit. When you realize that a problem or goal is unreachable at this time (for whatever reason), with a focused mind and a strong will you can turn your intention to another, more achievable goal while not obsessing on this unfinished task. A strong will gives you the ability to stop.

A PSYCHOLOGICAL NOTE

Gestalt psychology, among other systems, shows that people tend to return to uncompleted tasks or goals until they finish them or until they reach a place where they can let them go. In my process group I have found about 20-25% of a person's energy is typically wasted on useless worrying and revisiting of old goals. You will always revisit some old "unfinished business," but with mindful awareness of your present goals and activities reinforced by Intention and Will, you spend considerably less time and energy on the irrelevant and obsolete.

How do you develop an Iron Will? As I've said previously, Will is a primal force that exists within you at birth. Our task is to focus it and not allow continuous random activities to dissipate its power. I have found the big four killers of Will are limited awareness, undue stress, premature judgment and becoming tied to results rather than the process. By now I hope you see that all four are interconnected; therefore, to address any one of them, you must address all of them!

I've talked about all four of them at length, but the fourth factor, process orientation, bears repeating and repeating and repeating and repeating. Remember, goals are just identified steps in your overall strategy for a brilliant life. As new information becomes available, you should modify these goals/steps. Goal should be 80% about process and only 20% about the end result. Yes, the result is important, but the journey is what is truly important. This journey is your life. This journey is your life. This journey is your life.

If you focus on the results alone, you will miss the good parts. For example, from their birth, I envisioned to seeing my children graduate from high school and then college, but what would I have missed if I had just focused on that end result? Seeing them graduate was a wonderful result that I will treasure the rest of my life; however, their graduation pales to insignificance when compared to all the highs and lows it took to get to that place. Don't cheat yourself out of your life by focusing exclusively on results.

Another key reason for developing a process orientation to life is that it encourages mindfulness which, as new information becomes available, allows you to refine and improve your results. Decisions flow from an organic, interactive process. Think about the importance of this for a moment: by being mindfully present and withholding premature judgment, new, useful information will usually appear without effort. Of equal importance is the savings in time and stress.

No one can anticipate every factor, every change in dynamics, but everyone can develop the ability to adapt. My mental role model is a battlefield commander. I set my plan into motion and carefully observe the results as they happen. I am careful not to judge the results prematurely, nor to wait too long when I see things going to H——, but this is only possible if I stay centered and balanced and in the present moment. You'll find that this style of handling the tasks of life is both invigorating and relatively low stress. But honestly, I must admit the real reason I have adapted to this style of living is the time savings. A little tactical planning, throw in some power of Intention and set the plan in motion.

By now I hope you can see the insidious downside of being focused exclusively on results. People who are exclusively focused on results may be more successful at getting to a specific goal, but they get nothing else for their efforts and lose much along the way. They become rigid and myopic, missing out on large parts of the great story that is their life and developing no new skills or new brilliant goals.

An added bonus of process orientation is that discovering the next steps in your life journey is a relatively stress-free quest that concurrently refines the very skills you will need to complete those future steps successfully. Double bang!

My Iron Will and Intention formula for successfully reaching life goals...

- Dream it, feel it, see it
- Spend the time to make it feel real
- If it's worth doing, it is worth planning
- Don't be afraid to ask for advice
- Being an adult means admitting we don't know everything
- Write it down
- Be specific about all necessary steps
- Allocate all necessary resources

- Make sure you allocate sufficient time to this task
- Verify or modify your overall life plan to include this goal
- Make all goals and sub-goals measurable
- Achievable
- Balance the risk
- Timely—set a time limit on the overall task and its sub steps
- Make sure you are congruent in mind and body
- Meditate, pray or reflect on this goal
- If this is an important task or goal is of reasonably short duration, stay focused on it alone
- Multi-tasking isn't very effective for life goals
- eliminate or delay working on other goals whenever possible
- Use the power of "no"
- Get help from other people when needed
- Invoke the power of Intention
- Build energy
- Write a ritual and perform it
- Use affirmations
- Try self hypnotism
- Meditate, pray or reflect on it
- Have a formal kickoff event
- Don't start until you are ready
- Make the kickoff memorable
- Do something that is a concrete, measurable step towards completing this goal and celebrate it
- Update your records as you complete subtasks
- Celebrate the journey, both the good and the bad
- Whenever necessary, invoke the power of Will to carry you forward
- Watch out for stress
- Don't over-manage the details
- Watch out for expectations that limit your vision

- Avoid the blame game when things go wrong
- Because it can go wrong
- Because it will go wrong
- If you're blaming, you're not learning
- Know when to quit; do it mindfully with firmly developed criteria and reasons
- Ritualize, reflect and record, don't let it die with a whimper
- Honor the attempt and celebrate what you've learned
- Is it time to take a rest?
- Never tie your self-esteem and self image to your goals— you are not your goals
- Win or lose, don't let your goals define you
- Anytime you complete a goal, great or small, take some time to internalize the ramifications
- Record it and review
- Celebrate it
- Find time to rest and recharge
- Begin focus on the next task
- Revise your strategy as necessary

A USEFUL STORY

A poor farmer in the 16th century, who lived in a frontier province of China, had only three things of value: a beautiful white mare, a loving wife and a strong son. One day the mare ran off to the wild frontier. His neighbors all said what a terrible thing this was. He said, "Is it?" A week later the mare returned with two stallions and his neighbors said, "What a wonderful blessing!" And he said, "Is it?" The following day his only son attempted to tame the stallions and broke his leg. His neighbors all said, "What terrible misfortune." He said, "Is it?" A week later an army of bandits descended on his village and press ganged all the able young man into their bandit army.

Building Trust and Self-Trust

BRILLIANT LIVES ARE composed of a web of complex relationships, nurturing, fulfilling relationships with oneself and others. Relationships need to be based on authentic trust. I'm going to refrain from defining authentic trust until I've clearly defined what I mean by trusting relationships, but let's be clear from the beginning that trust is a choice. It's not some organic drive or even acknowledged as important to a good life—it is! Nietzsche pointed out that what is closest to us is often farthest from our awareness and trust/distrust is that type of in-your-face-all-the-time-so-you- don't-notice-it-anymore aspect of our lives. When I work with people in group I've noticed that the only time trust is mentioned is when it's been violated. Kind of like air quality, you only notice it when it's bad and you can't breathe.

I define three basic types of trust: basic trust, authentic trust and stupid-ass trust. Basic trust is naive trust. It's trust that it's never been challenged or looked at or violated. It's the trust between a mother and her child and the type of trust that the advertising world tries to foster on you when they're trying to sell your products. In contrast, authentic trust is based on reasonable limits and is cultivated over time by meeting commitments. Authentic trust, a core aspect of any healthy relationship, requires constant reinforcement, maintenance and a commitment to open communication. Stupid-ass trust is the abdication of choice.

Rather than think for yourself you willfully give that choice to some other entity, be it a government, a religion or a talk radio host—it doesn't matter because you have given away your right to think for yourself.

Over a period of years I've come to believe that a lack of trust is now the number one cause of dysfunctional relationships and organizations. Obviously if you can't trust someone it's awful hard to communicate honestly with that person because honest communication involves vulnerability and you don't want to be vulnerable with somebody you can't trust. In previous chapters I discussed how mindfulness and living in the moment help us control the bombardment of expectations we receive from society at large and in our personal relationships. Trust plays an important part in this interface, too. Trust determines—or it should determine—the porosity of your personal boundaries.

Authentic trust leads to clean boundaries and clear understanding of your beliefs and feelings before and after you have digested new material. The buffoon's uncritical absorption of information leads to self-deception.

Why do I believe authentic trust has given way to stupid-ass trust in the modern world? Frankly, I think it's that most people don't trust themselves. And they're not capable of self trust because they are so busy just trying to survive that they don't have time to develop those aspects of themselves that lead to the self-esteem and self-awareness that are essential to self-trust. And, without real self-esteem, the Ego will take command of the ship that is your being. Ego is your internal cop who has ingested the beliefs and goals of society—much of them before you were out of diapers. And Ego, like any good cop, is about punishment, reward and the avoidance of risk. Freedom of choice makes self-trust a big threat to the Ego because a loss of predictability is perceived as risk is—Ego freak out time! So it's the job of Ego (society's internal controller) to limit our choices to those society favors. Making self-esteem dependent on the rewards of society is the easiest way to accomplish this. Typically, "Cop shows" use a variant of "good cop, bad cop" to manipulate people into doing what they want them to do. Society manipulates you with even more "bad cop, worst cop." The bad cop is society telling you what to do by playing on your fears and anxieties. And the worst cop is your Ego telling you not to listen to your heart and mind, but listen to society's propaganda instead. They are a formidable set of opponents, because, even though their expectations are externally imposed, they are often correct.

So, while we can't ignore the messages society imposes on us, we must always remember to mindfully digest the messages before acting on them. Your Ego definitely doesn't want you to live with mindful awareness because that could lead to self-esteem, the basis for authentic self-trust and freedom of choice.

Have you noticed how our world is becoming increasingly more complex, more global, and more technologically opaque? We have become dependent on devices such as computers and cell phones which are incomprehensible "black boxes." We need loads of trust to live in our modern world. Unfortunately, these devices don't always function correctly, so if you have tied your self-esteem and personal identity to these devices, then you will perceive yourself as not functioning—ouch! But don't worry. Your Ego and society will bail you out. Your Ego will roll out the excuses and society will trot out technological solutions that really solve nothing.

However, if you operate on the basis of self-esteem, mindfulness, acceptance and a phenomenological perspective, the failure of one of these "black boxes" will have minimal impact on your life. I'm not saying it will have zero impact, but it should be pretty minimal. My favorite example of technological fallibility is cable television. Why does it seem that the cable always goes out during the big game? Hmmmm...

Another aspect of our modern world that freaks me out is the doubling of our knowledge base every seven years. It's nearly impossible to stay abreast of the new discoveries in one's chosen field of expertise. It is impossible to be knowledgeable about all the things our lives now depend on. That leaves two choices: trust yourself or drop out of the race for a brilliant life.

Sadly, most people choose option two. If they did it willfully, I could accept it, but most people choose the path of least resistance unconsciously and that is very sad. If you let society dictate your beliefs and goals, you don't even know you have a right to choose to change. When I was in college, I was often confronted with these two choices and, like a good science major, when I realized I couldn't put this stuff into finite equations, I ran like hell in the opposite direction. At the time I didn't realize that making no decision was a decision, a decision to adapt to the default choice—dropout and let other people make my decisions—stupid ass trust.

How are the two choices different? Both surrender trying to understand the technological systems we're embedded in, but with choice one you reserve the right to change your mind about any part of that decision in the future. Even more significantly, choice one is typically limited to technological systems, whereas, choice two usually involves surrendering awareness of social, political and personal processes as well.

Stress Management and Breathing

STRESS MANAGEMENT IN our complex world requires a mixture of techniques and commitment. Interesting fact: if a frog is dropped into a beaker of boiling water, it will jump out immediately. On the other hand, if you put a frog into a beaker of warm water and slowly raise the temperature, the frog will stay in there until it boils to death! Modern society is a lot like that. The stress has been slowly but continuously ratcheted up and we passively accept it. Are you boiling yet? What can you do?

Here are some basic truths:

1. There is no such thing as good stress.
2. Stress is generated both internally and externally.
3. Stress management has to be a priority to make it work.

It's time to get out your journal again and answer these questions.

- Are you living your beliefs?
- Are you making progress on financial independence?
- On a scale of one to 10, how is your self acceptance?
- Are you taking any downtime?
- Are you getting exercise?
- Are friends and family supportive of your life goals?

I realize I'm making you answer the same questions again and again and again, but each time it's from a different perspective that will help you realize your brilliant life.

Now, I'd like to discuss a few stress management techniques that might save your life:

- Correct breathing
- Meditation/prayer/reflection
- Mindful acceptance of the life's changes

I became an engineering manager in the 1980s. By the 90s I had high blood pressure. My doctor told me I was you're going to die—or worse—if I didn't change my lifestyle. You would think that threat would've been a great motivator, but it wasn't. Sure, I put a plan together of external changes. I cut out 80% of the red meat in my diet and dropped 30 pounds; I switched from weightlifting to basketball as my primary exercise and added in walking...it didn't change a thing! The blood pressure dropped a little, not enough, and it still shot to the moon with any extended pressure at work. Internally I was still wound tighter than a long-tailed cat in a room full of rocking chairs. I was a bomb primed to go off.

And it did when my start-up company died! It nearly killed me and saved my life at the same time. When the blackness of severe depression hit, I was a poster child for overwork, overstress and hypertension, but I had zero awareness of these facts. I turned from being a "successful" entrepreneurial engineer to a numb lump of failure overnight. The couch, the TV and Hostess cupcakes became my only friends (a real pity party), but I was able to rise from the ashes of my life by looking at my life...I realized I had never put any energy into it. I had put all my energy, my life energy into my work. Further, I realized I had no tools to help me out of this predicament, but I did have a loving wife, my key support system. She got me on the road—a new road—to building a better life. It's not an overnight process. When you fall down that hard and you don't have any tools to help you, it's going to be a long climb. So that's what this chapter is really about is giving you the tools to avoid becoming Hostess cupcakes' number one customer—and maybe save your life.

When I was finally capable of returning to engineering, I took a job with less stress. That helped. Taking regular vacations helped. Joining a process group seemed to help a lot. But what helped most was a combination of all the above: learning to breathe correctly, to mediate daily and to live with mindful awareness. My health and my attitude really started to improve, but I wasn't in the clear yet. I was still getting stressed, but I was learning to handle the pressure better. Still, I needed a laxative now and then and I still had problems sleeping if I was stressed for extended periods of time. I needed to make more changes.

Luckily my reactions to stress pinpointed the flaws in my current lifestyle. I'd made tremendous progress but I hadn't gone far enough. I was breathing much better now and with my twenty- minute meditation sessions every morning, I began to feel much more balanced and clear minded. Yet, I was still suffering from bouts of hypertension. Why? Because I haven't completed the deal. I had not made the key change. I still thought of stress as a foreign enemy and not an element of my personal ecosystem. Stress has become part of nearly everything we do these days.

What is stress, really? Think of a recent event in your life that was stressful. How did it make you feel? Now, think of a time when you were in serious pain. Remember how that felt. Now compare the two. Right, they feel quite similar because they are! Stress is pain with a thick veneer of self-doubt. Common effects include self-hatred and the loss of a sense of personal responsibility.

Where does stress originate? My personal opinion is stress moved near the top of the hierarchy of pain when we started to live by the clock. Clock time now dominates the flow of our lives.

In our present-day corporate world, working by the clock allows us to interact more effectively with our fellow human beings. Some of life's functions will always be controlled by clock time—doctor appointments, school, movie schedules, etc. The problem starts when we allow clock time to control all aspects of our lives, because we're trying to do too much! I don't know about you, but if I try to do too much in too short a time, I tend to compromise the quality because I'm worrying about not getting tasks done on time. Another major drawback is that I'm not fully present to the activity at hand, for I have become fixated on my time fears and anxieties. When you over schedule, you can't be mindfully present because you are always feeling stressed about staying on schedule.

Think about this process for a moment. We have a task that is probably partially dependent on other people to accomplish, but we pretend that we have complete control of it. Hardly! Remember, we are small components of a complex, endlessly interacting system that has its own objectives and schedules. Sometimes we catch a break and the present task is adequately isolated from the larger systems that surround us that we can exert a reasonable amount of control over the process. Typically, we won't know if this is true or not until we are deep into the task. Usually, however, we aren't adequately aligned with or isolated from these systems, which makes us strongly dependent on other people to get the task completed. In our hierarchical, corporate world we don't even decide the amount of time to allocate for completing this task—a double whammy!

Freud and his kindred claimed that time management relates to our desire to control death. Heavy, but there is more than a little truth in that statement. Death is anti-gene propagation, so "avoiding death" perches near the top of the hierarchy of hardwired biological programs. So, you can see how anything that increases the probability of death will increase the stress level, given our hardwiring. It also works the other way. Stress evokes deep, unconscious fears of death. So, a little stress from any source with tend to shut down our higher processes and put us in a survival mode—fight or flight—and leave us wide-open to manipulation. Don't doubt for a moment that the various institutions of this modern world are using stress daily to control and manipulate you.

You know the drill: "Act now, or you'll miss this time-limited opportunity!" So what can you do? Let me restate the formula that has worked for me.

My Stop Stress Now formula:

1. Don't over schedule!
2. Meditate or pray daily
3. Exercise regularly
4. Laugh a lot
5. Learn non-attachment to results
6. See the world from a phenomenological, nonjudgmental perspective
7. Outsource everything non-essential that you can afford
8. Consciously learn to recognize when you're not breathing and take a couple conscious full, deep breaths
9. Align your world as much as possible with your goals and beliefs

Who thought stress reduction would be so complicated? It's so complicated because of how ingrained it is an everyday reality, but it doesn't have to be a big part of your reality. Stress is going to happen, so don't be like the frog. Be aware and actively root it out.

The easiest and fastest way I have found to reduce stress is breathing. The best way to experience the positive effect of breathing is to experience it.

Let me ask you to take a moment and observe your breathing....

Don't try to influence it. Just observe. Are you breathing high from your chest or low from your belly? Are your breaths deep, slow and complete or shallow and fast? A complete breath starts below the navel and fully inflates the lower belly. After your lower belly is comfortably full and fully expanded, air should start filling the chest. And when your chest is full, let the air exit slowly and evenly from your lungs through your nose. Your exhalation should start from the top of the chest and move smoothly down into your belly and pelvis.

• Your exhalation should be smooth, slow and complete.
• Your exhalation should be smooth, slow and complete.
• Your exhalation should be smooth, slow and complete.

I have found it instructive to place one hand on my stomach and in the other on my chest to get feedback about the extent and order of my inhalations and exhalations. Let's try this together. Place your hands on your chest and stomach and inhale slowly, focusing on inflating the lower part of your lungs. Observe how your belly and sides begins to rise with this breath. If you're belly doesn't expand, take a moment to consciously relax your abdominal region. Good breathing requires a relaxed thorax and abdomen. Your breathing will improve immensely just by doing this alone. Okay, assuming you've relaxed your stomach and your chest, let them expand from the pelvis to the collarbones. Your breath should be slow, smooth, deep and regular. I have found nothing better to keep stress from growing to massive proportions than taking a few slow, deep, smooth and regular breaths when faced with a traumatic situation. All kinds of useful breathing patterns and techniques exist for you to explore and add to your repertoire. In the appendix I have included a number of useful references to aid you in your exploration.

Breathing and stress are intimately tied together. I've found that if my breathing is relaxed, my body and my mind are also relaxed.

My blood pressure stays down and my higher-level neo-cortex functions don't get shoved aside by hardwired survival mechanisms. It's my belief that the stress that dominates our modern lives is compromising our health. You would think we would all have Ph.D.'s in correct breathing, but I'm willing to bet that the majority of people reading this book have never even considered developing or needing a "Breathing Right Program." I know I thought I didn't need one, but hypertension and sleep problems taught me otherwise.

My breathing-for-stress-relief program is simple but effective. I use a basic NLP (neurolinguistic programming) technique called "anchoring" to make me automatically check my breathing. At the top of every hour I take four deep, slow breaths making sure my exhalation is longer than my inhalation. If no one is around, I take four more deep breaths through my nose, and I exhale with a soft, smooth audible sigh. I also check my breathing any time I hear my name or read or write an e-mail. With a little practice it becomes automatic. You may find it useful to have the computer beep at the top of every hour if you work at a desk...I also practice breathing correctly while repeating my name to myself several times a day.

What else can you do when the stress monster calls?

When stress calls, make sure you have a well-practiced stress management process in place. Stress management is analogous to an Army field hospital.

First, you stop the bleeding and determine the extent of the injury. I'm sure I'm not the first person to tell you that, when the stress monster hits you upside the head, it's usually a good move to step back and take a look at the big picture.

Step One: Take a couple of deep breaths. Put all your previous experiences on hold.

Step Two: Concentrate on the information coming from your senses and not just your conscious mind. Listen to your body and feel what it is telling you. Open yourself to the complete experience of what's being presented to you—reject nothing!!!

Step Three: Describe the situation without judgment. Describe it without any cause and effect statements and without prioritizing. Don't favor the aspects that you perceive as good over the seemingly bad or the neutral qualities. Embrace them all equally at this point.

Step Four: Integrate your thoughts and feelings and allow them to rise to your conscious awareness. Breathe into and relax with the various aspects of the situation. Let a new whole vision emerge, a new gestalt.

Step Five: Don't rush yourself. Let it emerge organically. In our modern world you're always going to get pushed to respond now. Very rarely is it truly necessary. In the business world I frequently buy myself time to consider my response fully. "I'll get back to you when I get the information "is one of my favorites. Some other favorites include cleaning my glasses, taking a sip water and—my all-time favorite—getting out a sheet of paper to make a note. These methods serve to give you a few seconds to breathe and relax, to gather your thoughts so you respond in a way authentic to your beliefs and understanding.

At this point you should be able to deal with the majority of your stress and anxiety. If major residual feelings or stressful thoughts remain, repeat the process until you're comfortable.

Step Six: Complete the experience and let it go. If it's time to think-THINK! Complete your analysis and decide on your course of action or non-action. If you do this, I know you will greatly reduce your stress. If it's time to act-ACT! Commit whole heartily and don't second guess yourself. There will be time afterward to analysis your decision. By committing to the chosen path with a clear focused intent your body can stay relaxed; your mind quiet and your perceptions will be a balance of external and internal stimuli. And you will be in the best position to response effectively.

I've read that ancient Japanese samurai could compose haiku in the middle of a duel because they could balance the "noise" of external stimuli with a quiet mind. I hope someday get to that point, but for now, I'm happy to remember to breathe and follow my process. Even if I just remember to breathe, I find I have the energy to react and do. Remember, the unconscious (some people call it the out-of-conscious) mind has a great deal more computational horsepower than the conscious mind and there's no better time to use that resource than in the middle of a crisis.

The key factors that allowed the samurai to balance the external and internal were practice and meditation. Shouldn't we do the same? If it worked for them, it will work for you. Firemen and soldiers practice their skills all the time (and I wish they would meditate regularly, too, but....) Anyway, I know that if you meditate regularly, in the middle of a crisis you will be more centered and balanced. Yes, you may be scared sh**less, like any soldier in the middle of battle, but constant practice will help you learn to control the fear and react more effectively. A strange argument I've heard against daily meditation and/or prayer is that it takes time. Abraham Lincoln said, "If I have eight hours to chop down a tree, I will spend six hours sharpening my ax." He's absolutely correct, and the payback is enormous. The second argument I've heard against meditating daily is that our ancestors didn't need it, so why should we? Of course, they didn't need to learn to drive or use a computer, either. Different times require different tools.

In the final analysis, it's the work you do before a major

stressful event that is the real secret to handling stress successfully. I hope you decide to use all these techniques, but I know 80% of your stress will disappear—like magic—if you adopt an open phenomenological perspective and work on your breathing.

Time Management and Personal Power

I'VE READ MANY books on time management and most of the techniques mentioned are quite valid and useful, but they miss the point. They are about improving work efficiency only and not about living better. Improving your time management skills has turned into trying to cram too many things into too little time. It's a symptom of the disease I call "24/7-itis." Real time management should be about decreasing the time you need to work while increasing the time you have to live.

Many of the best time-management books' methodologies—if applied without mindfulness—will lead you to a dead end. They trumpet that the core principle of time management is saving time. Wrong!

It should be about maximum effectiveness. I think they encourage this approach because saving clock time is measurable, whereas effectiveness is more global and therefore harder to quantify in the short term.

They also totally ignore the very human paradox for realizing max efficiency is LAZINESS. I think Julie Newmar said it best:

> *On Sundays, I like to concentrate on laziness. It's*
> *absolutely paramount if you want to be a Monday*
> *dynamo.*

Right now, sit down with your notebook and write down all your time commitments. I'm sure you have a ton more than this, but the list should include:

1. Working
2. Commuting
3. Sleeping
4. Eating (at home)
5. Watching TV (average time)
6. Operating the computer (average time)
7. Attending church/temple/mosque
8. Getting exercise
9. Instigating bedroom maneuvers (you figure it out)
10. Enjoying recreation (dining, movies, hobbies)
11. Vacationing
12. Meditating, praying, reflecting
13. Reading
14. Helping the kids with homework
15. Paying bills, doing chores
16. Shopping
17. Taking a class
18. Planning for the future
19. Playing with the kids
20. Paying attention to your loved ones
21. Respect additional time commitments

How does it look? I would bet you're overcommitted by a factor of three to four times the available time.

Now prioritize the list!!!

Write it down!!

Spend some time thinking about it!

QUESTIONS

- Where are you spending the bulk of your time?
- Are your time commitments congruent with your values and beliefs?
- Do you have any time to pursue your interests?
- What can you eliminate?

This last one is a toughie. It's tough because "they" want you to think he don't have any control. In the beginning it's pretty much the truth because you've given away much of your personal power to the systems that you were born into. You can take back a portion of that power and get back some control, but not all of it, because it is to your advantage to stay vested [partially] in these systems.

How do you get back some of the power and achieve balance?

To do this you will need to apply the previously discussed techniques of mindfulness, breathing, the power of no, and a non-judgmental perspective. The goal of these techniques is to erect a selectively porous barrier around all of your various emotional and intellectual interactions. This barrier gives you the means to control the bombardment of your senses from society, family and friends without either ignoring them or non-critically ingesting them. The combination of these tools will create a safe zone between you and the world, allowing you to process the multitude of stimuli you are constantly receiving. I think about these three as my version of the Matrix movie slow-motion bullet dodging. In truth, these three methods are just different aspects of the same intention- to find the time and space to think, feel, and decide.

Like the Matrix movies, life isn't what it appears to be; however, by living with awareness, embracing a phenomenological perspective, and giving yourself time and space to breathe and relax, you can find the meaning behind the appearance. I devote separate chapters to each of these topics because they are easier to discuss that way, but in reality they are not separate. They're all interrelated with multiple, intertwining feedback loops uniting them. From the moment of birth we are all thrown into a complex system of interactive processes that want our constant attention—don't yield!

Think about it: if you're completely tied into these processes and systems, no "you" exists other than what is these systems define—Ouch!

Realistically, we're all defined to a large extent, both internally and externally, by these systems. And that's a good thing if you are embedded in a worthy system that fit with your values and beliefs.

Accept the truth that your "ecosystem" of relationships structures a large part of your world. Given that this is true, is your ecosystem healthy and positive?

QUESTIONS TO CONSIDER

- Does your ecosystem support your goals and life direction?
- What are your key support systems?
- What is your principal style of communication within this system?
- What parts of your life are you satisfied with?
- What parts of your life are you dissatisfied with?

KEY EXERCIZE

Now, within both the good and bad aspects of your life, identify those areas where you have given up your personal power. How did it happen? If you don't know (and I bet you don't), make up a story. It will probably contain the reasons you gave up control. You'll find some of the reasons quite valid while others will violate your beliefs and values. It's important that you treat both sides of any issue equally without pre-judgment if you truly want to understand how you lost your power.

- Write it down in your journal.
- Write it down in your journal.
- Write it down in your journal.

As a engineering manager, I used to think "more is better." I was completely wrong. Personal efficiency and, more importantly, decision-making ability drop precipitously after working more than four continuous hours. A little break, a little exercise, and a little conversation can really recharge your batteries. Not a fifteen-minute cigarette break or a rushed lunch break filled with talk about work, but a real separation. One advantage of living in California is that nearly every day I can walk down to the basketball court or take my car to a driving range and hit a bucket of balls and separate myself totally from my job for 30 to 45 minutes. A third option that I seem to avail myself of more and more lately is to walk over to Borders Café with my MP3 player. My niece works in the music business here and puts together some really eclectic song lists for me. I plug in my headphones, turn on the music, relax and breathe. I also consciously check in with my body and look for stress and rigidity. I usually finish off all three of these activities with the bottle of water and an energy bar.

Contrary to what you might believe, this hour is the best spent time of my workday. It's during this time I regain my balance and center. All the techniques in this book are aimed at helping you maintain your center and balance, but realistically they're going to be days (weeks) where one incident after another that will challenge you to remember to take a bathroom break and a deep breath now and then. It's particularly important on those days that you separate yourself both mentally and physically from the battle at regular intervals. What does this have to do with time management?

What do my three favorite break time activities have in common? First, all three activities put me in the moment. Secondly, my job makes me live in my head, so when I'm on break, I need to relate to my body. Thirdly, all three of them give me personal space. All three activities still bombard me with perceptual stimuli, but they're now at a slower pace and are more predictable. Hmmmm, maybe I should consider adding a fourth activity of a bit of stretching, tai chi and breathing meditation. And alternate that with a nap. Checking in with my body as I write this, I'm sensing strong agreement with these additions to my normal routine.

You probably consider me crazy, but I know I'm not because I've seen the results for me and the other people I've persuaded to try these techniques. Simply by learning to say no, taking real breaks, and making the commitment to laziness will greatly improve the amount of time you have for living. It's funny—you hear it all the time—"you have to spend money to make money," but if you spend time on anything that isn't labeled productive, you think you've committed a heinous act—go figure. There is a caveat to this plan. If you're massively overcommitted time-wise nothing is going to help you in the long run. Okay enough preaching. Let's move on to the techniques I've found most useful to further minimize the time you need to get your work done.

In work and life the number-one technique for improving productivity and efficiency is learning to say "NO".

- This isn't a macho thing. Please do it respectfully and courteously.
- The "no" we're talking about doesn't mean never. It means not right now.

We're bombarded daily with requests that interfere with what we're trying to accomplish at that time, yet we let others' priorities often override our own.-We need to learn to just say "no."

Stephen Covey's book *The Seven Habits of Highly Successful People* has a wonderful time management matrix that can teach you distinguish between urgent tasks, important tasks and those ol' 'round tuits.' When you learn to prioritize your tasks according to their importance to the fulfillment of your current goal, your decision making will really improve And, when you understand which tasks require immediate focus, you can be sure you're making the best use of your time. The power of "no" is particularly important with these prioritized tasks because to be most effective, you need to focus on that task exclusively. Multitasking has its place, but it has a brutal 'time overhead' associated with switching tasks. Don't do it unless it's absolutely necessary.

KEY POINT

Think results, not activities, and plan accordingly.

GET FOCUSED

Start each day making a list of your priorities for that day. It should be a short list of no more than five items. Probably some of the items will come from your list from yesterday. It's vitally important that you begin every work day reviewing what went on yesterday and understand why some items from yesterday didn't get completed. Was it because priorities changed or because you lost focus, figured it out and corrected it. This shouldn't be a long process (15 minutes tops), but it is immeasurably important. It doesn't matter how you keep your list. I prefer a yellow legal pad.

Other choices include a little pocket notebook or Microsoft Outlook. What's right is what works for you.

Keep a separate list of all tasks and update it several times a day as a new tasks and priorities come in. I find it useful to circle in red new tasks that have high importance. And don't be afraid to eliminate any tasks that are irrelevant. Some people I've gotten to do this also list these items with estimated completion times. I think that's a useful addition to this process, but it's not something I've adopted yet-hopefully soon.

KEY POINT

Always, always, always do the things first that will get you the biggest bang for your time.

DECISION-MAKING IN THE INFORMATION AGE

It's true; we do live in an Information Age. Information is only useful, though, only if it is relevant to the task at hand and only after it's been scrutinized (consciously and subconsciously, without pre-judgment) and synthesized (mind and body) with the rest of your knowledge (beliefs and goals). Don't confuse information with knowledge. I used to believe that I should always gather as much information as possible and then sort it and synthesize it. That doesn't work anymore because there's just too much information and much of it is not reliable. Always take the time to gather useful information from diverse sources and take particular care to find information on both sides of the issue at hand. Don't be one of those people who filter out information that is contrary to their beliefs. Once you've gathered all relevant information, apply phenomenological analysis rigorously. Good judgment is the natural product of this analysis if you commit to it.

How does this relate to time management? Very straightforwardly. If you know the importance of the decision you are making, you can allocate sufficient time to make a good decision within the context of your overall priorities. If it's in an important decision, give it the time and resources it merits. If it's a minor decision with minor consequences, minimize the information-gathering process and the decision-making criteria and the time commitment. But always use a phenomenological perspective to help you arrive at your final decision. There are some very useful tools available for helping you make decisions, but they would require their own book to adequately cover them. I list several excellent books that cover this subject in Appendix A. Before I end this section, I want to mention one strategy that I have found particularly useful in life planning. The neurolinguistic psychological method (NLP) technique called the "TOTE" method: Test-Operate-Test-Exit.

The TOTE method for making decisions is a closed-loop decision-making process that involves six steps.

1. As clearly as possible, define the problem and the outcome you desire.

2. Test the desired outcome against the current situation.

3. Select the approach to solving this problem and execute it.

4. Test the outcome of this process against your desired result.

5. If the result is sufficient, proceed to your exit strategy; otherwise, repeat steps one through four as needed.

6. Verify that your solution was implemented as you desired and let it go.

Every good decision-making process has these basic steps embedded in it. Most people are good at steps two through five, but take shortcuts with steps one and six. Don't do it! If you do step one correctly, I guarantee your decision-making skills will show a quantum improvement.

Step six is also very important because you are often dependent on other people to implement your solutions, and that situation can cause you two more problems. Problem one is obvious: your solution doesn't get implemented correctly. Problem two is quieter and more insidious: if you don't check on the progress and outcome of your proposed solution, how will you know when it's done? It's hard to let it go if you don't know. Always include checking on your results as part of your "to-do list."

DEATH BY EMAIL

Another common time killer is excessive reading and responding to email. I won't even mention people who are addicted to their Blackberry (We call it "Crackberry" in Silicon Valley). It's another symptom of 24/7-itis. If it is really important, the person should call you or meet you face-to-face. Unfortunately, many people are so overloaded that they use email as a means to communicate when other means are more appropriate. Yes, you probably do need to spend a fair amount of time with email, but do it in a structured way.

Whether at home or at the office, you should first prepare your to- do list and set the day's priorities. Now, spend thirty minutes checking and responding to your email. At this point you may want me to revisit your to-do list and, of course, update as needed. If possible, assign a priority rating to all these new tasks.

At fixed intervals only (two hours minimum) check your email. Spend no more than fifteen minutes reading and corresponding to these emails. You don't have to read every one of them. If they're not relevant, trash them instantly. Sort all the other ones by priority and interest. I've set up ten folders in my e-mail account labeled with priority level, interest and project information.

An important folder I've added recently is my follow-up folder. My follow-up folder has really improved my organizational abilities. As part of my morning routine I always check and update this file now. It's really easy—once you get in the habit—to place a copy of all pending commitments and obligations in this folder. I just wish I could color code them, too.

JUST FINISH ONE THING

Make it your standard operating procedure to start with your highest priority and work on one thing at a time Always define measurable sub-goals, or interim steps, that you can accomplish every day for each of your important projects. Life projects in particular extend over long periods of time, so it is vital that you make progress regularly, or you will lose focus. I'm not saying you have work daily on all your life projects, but regularity is necessary if you want to keep a momentum in accomplishing these projects.

Work projects are another story. Here, daily results are a must. If you can't accomplish some important (a two-minute call to check on progress with all team members, for example) and have to focus on sub-tasks for of all your projects every day, then you have too many projects and you need to delegate some of them. Delegation isn't that tough if you understand your priorities and what you and others are best at doing.

Delegation isn't a power game. It's about maximizing efficiency and productivity at work and at home. Many tasks in your life you don't need to do, you are not suited for, or that don't make the best use of your time. I have a yard and a garden. I love to work in my garden, but yard maintenance limits the time available for my garden. Answer? I hired the boy next door to weed, water, and mow my yard. He makes a few dollars, his parents are happy because he's learning responsibility, and I'm happy because I have more time for my garden.

At work, delegation is an art because everybody is overloaded. I had problems trying to raise other people to my level in order to lift some of my work load even when I was willing to take on some of their tasks in return. Then, I realized I was going about it the wrong way—logically. Logic tends not to work with overstressed people, so I changed my strategy and appealed to their self-interest. The results were immediate.

Delegation at work and at home has a wonderful upside because it forces you evaluate your priorities and interests in light of those of the other people. If for no other reason, you should regularly delegate one of your tasks to really make yourself see other people and their interests free of your own expectations and desires.

FOR MAXIMUM TM

- Practice Just-in-Time information gathering
- Use email correctly
- Minimize interruptions
- Always have a to-do list
- Do one thing at a time
- Learn to delegate
- TOTE it-test, operate, test and exit

Developing Your Strategy for a Brilliant Life

THIS CHAPTER IS really a rehash of everything I've said before mixed in a (hopefully) coherent synthesis.

Step one: taking control of your finances.

- How much do you owe?
- How are you spending from your income?
- How much are you saving?
- What would happen if you lost your job?
- What are your short-term and long-term financial goals?
- What can you do today to move toward them?

It might seem strange that I have started this last chapter of the book pushing financial planning again, but my reason is quite simple. In this modern society, if you don't control your money, it will certainly control you! Money is the tool most of the people of Earth have chosen for the exchange of goods, services and Time.

Yes, money is really about time. As working stiffs we exchange our life energy and time for money, money that pays for the things we want in our life. But if we allow the pursuit of money to dominate our time, we will have no life. How do we find the balance? It's a complex process that starts with assessing your present financial status. Over a 90-day period, record every expense and start a real savings account. Don't develop your "final" budget yet. You have important decisions to make before you get to that point. Concurrent with this process you should also keep a time commitment journal. How are you really spending your time? I'll bet you will be surprised. Additionally, it's time to commit to adding a short quiet period (20 minutes of meditation, prayer or contemplation) to your already hectic schedule.

KEY QUESTIONS TO THINK ABOUT

- What are my beliefs?
- What are my key goals?
- How do I want to spend my life?
- Is my present life congruent with my beliefs, goals and needs?
- Where are my car keys?

Along with these questions also consider the questions in the earlier chapters. But remember, during this process you should spend time just sitting and breathing. Be quiet and allow yourself to connect with higher powers—you know, life, the universe and everything. Okay, a bit much to ask. perhaps. How about connecting with yourself and developing a quiet, critic-free mind? Sounds simple, but it will probably take you a lifetime to achieve, the payoff is astronomical.

Game time! With the insights you have gathered from these 90 days of recording your spending habits and time commitments, it's time to develop the Grand Strategy. Really put some effort into this process. Document all your life goals and objectives. Write them up in detail. With each objective and goal develop a tactical approach you can use to get there. Then, develop a complete, but flexible, timeline. Set up a series of periodic reviews and revisit and revise your tactics and goals as new information becomes available.

KEY POINTS

- Don't expect to get this done in an evening or a weekend. It may take months.
- Remember the Prieto principle.
- Prioritizing will gain you the biggest improvement.
- Gather information from all the important people in your life.
- Ask lots of questions.
- Don't try to be perfect.
- Dream big!
- Commit to being mindful of your goals and objectives.
- With each objective and goal develop a tactical approach you can use to get there.
- Develop a complete, but flexible, timeline.
- Set up a series of periodic reviews and revisit and revise your tactics and goals as new information becomes available.

Why is this process necessary? Simple.

Who do you want to use your life—you or someone else? Consider this: Columbus went looking for a trade route to the Orient, but what he found was so much more important. Talk about a man with an iron will! The years it took to get the voyage funded, his sailing into the unknown, and then his apparent failure—and he had the will to repeat the voyage. Could you do that? I'm willing to bet you could—if you integrate these processes in your life.

Now, with your strategy, tactics and goals clearly defined, bring the power of intention and will into the game. Leave your judgment and self-criticism on the bench. Enter the game like a

Tiger Woods, with an open, phenomenological perspective in order to mindfully adjust to any situation while being in touch with your body. Keep a quiet mind, and remember your strategic objectives. Tiger Woods has a great swing, a wonderful short game and he can putt better than almost anyone, but his real advantage lies in his mental toughness. He is truly a Western Zen master, a guru of self-mastery. And the key component of self-mastery is the ability to minimize stress during a crisis while maintaining a high of self-esteem. Can you imagine the high stress of playing on TV at the Masters and missing a three-foot putt?

How would you react? Tiger was visibly shaken for a moment, but by the next tee his head was up, he was breathing deeply and he proceeded to hit a golf ball 350 yards down the center of the fairway. After the round, he spent an extra twenty minutes practicing his putting.

The key point to get from this story is that adversity happens to everybody. The secret is to stay in the moment without judging yourself or your abilities. Accept the outcome and adjust. Trust yourself and the process! Tiger knew in his heart that he had done the best he could in that moment and that was enough.

Why, then did he practice putting for an extra twenty minutes if missing a putt hadn't affected his self-worth? Why? He practiced because it was an opportunity to refine and adjust his putting skills (Darn. That's that what my teachers meant when they said tests are a learning opportunity).

Tiger Woods continues to get better and better even with upheavals in his life. Even with a damaged knee, a wrenched back, an aging body—oh, yes, and a new wife and a baby—he somehow manages to keep improving. Yes, his game temporarily tapered off, but with time, coaching, and honest self appraisal, he has come back stronger and better. Tiger's game is definitely different, but it is also definitely better. I believe Tiger is a living example of what this book is trying to teach. To Tiger, being the best golfer the history of the sport is not about personal glory;

rather, it's his way of judging the effectiveness of his golf skills - not himself! He loves golf, but golf doesn't define him. He loves competition, but competition is not his whole identity. He uses competition and the challenges that accompany it to explore the many aspects of the being who is Tiger Woods.

ONE FINAL SUGGESTION FOR A BRILLIANT LIFE

Work on your weaknesses, but spend the majority of your time developing your strengths.

A personal example: I'll continue to work on my writing, but if I waited until it was really good (by that I mean perfect), I would never have written this book. Now that I am actually writing, I realize this book is my process, my way of working on my writing while allowing me to communicate something that I feel is a very important. If I wait until my writing is perfect, I might never be ready to share with you these concepts that will radically improve your life. Writing this book also has had the secondary effect of helping me synthesize and focus my thinking on these important topics and become even more committed to this journey of creating a brilliant life.

Always devote time to improving all things that directly affect your life, while being mindfully aware that they will probably improve only so much. Also, be aware that some of your strengths will only marginally improve, but at least one will improve tremendously with the correct effort. Will you discover it and have time to develop it completely? I don't know, but I do know that you can greatly improve the odds of that happening if you follow the processes and techniques explained in this book.

Let me share with you one more personal truth. If you asked me whether I follow all the processes and techniques in this book, I can answer "yes." I follow them because they have greatly improved my life, but I must also admit that I have previously used some techniques more rigorously than others. Sometimes I was off track on all of them. Happily, that doesn't happen often these days because I've made an authentic commitment to follow them. Authentic commitment means prioritizing your life such that you can follow ALL the techniques.

My process of getting to the place where I could completely commit has taken me several years, but it doesn't have to be that way for you. The intellectual aspects of this process were easy for me to adopt adapt. Analysis and planning I can do in my sleep, but integrating mind and body and being mindfully aware of the total world—not just the things that interest me—took a bit of time and effort. I've always had a strong will (okay, originally I often confused being hard ass stubborn with having a strong will), but sadly I never really understand the importance of focus and intention. We put gasoline in our cars, batteries in our toys, food in our body but most of us never stop to consider the crucial importance of putting energy into our dreams. Rev up your future!

Appendix A: Recommended Readings

THE FOLLOWING IS my rather eclectic recommended reading list. The books in this list range from simplistic, spoon-feeding graphic novels to serious scholarly works. They cover all the topics discussed in this book and I have listed them in no particular order because I don't want you to read them in any particular order. Follow your heart and read what calls you. A dear friend of mine told me that if you have a good book(s) and God you are never alone. I think she's nearly correct: she forgot about blind panic as a constant companion.

• The 25 Best Time Management Tools and Techniques, Pamela Dodd and Doug Sundheim
• Influence: The Psychology of Persuasion, Robert Cialdini
• Take Back your Time: How to Regain Control of Work, Information and Technology, Jan Jasper
• How to Get Control of Your Time and Your Life, Alan Lakein
• *Do It Now!*, Andy Bruce and Ken Langdon
• Strategic Planning for Dummies, Erica Olsen
• Managing For Results, Peter Drucker
• Smart Choices: A Practical Guide to Making Better Life Decisions, John S. Hammond, Ralph L. Keeney and Howard

Raiffa
- Leadership: Inspire, Liberate and Achieve, Tom Peters
- The Tipping Point: How Little Things Can Make a Big Difference, Malcolm Gladwell
- Wharton on Making Decisions, Stephen J. Hoch
- Critical Thinking: An Introduction to Basic Skills, William Hughes
- Critical Thinking: An Introduction, Alex Fisher
- Nonsense—Red Herrings, Straw Men and Sacred Cows: How We Abuse Logic in our Everyday Language, Robert J. Gula
- Seeing Systems: unlocking the mysteries of organizational life by Barry Oshry
- The Art of Systems Thinking: Essential Skills for Creativity and Problem-Solving, Joseph O'Connor and Ian McDermott
- Systems Thinking: Managing Chaos and Complexity, Jamshid Gharajedaghi
- Our Iceberg is Melting: Changing and Succeeding Under Any Conditions, John Kotter and Holger Rathgeber
- The Power of Focus by Jack Canfield, Mark Victor Hansen and Les Hewitt
- Self Leadership and The One Minute Manager: Increasing Effectiveness through Situational Self Leadership, Susan Fowler and Lawrence Hawkins
- Leadership and Self-Deception: Getting Out of the Box, Arbinger Institute
- *The One Minute Entrepreneur*, Ken Blanchard, Don Hutson and Ethan Willis
- *Zen for Beginners*, Judith Blackstone and Zoran Josipovic
- *Instant Zen*, Jim McMullan and Michael Levin
- White Collar Zen: Using Zen Principles to Overcome Obstacles and Achieve Your Career Goals, Stephen Heine
- The Vision of The Buddha, Tom Lowenstein
- *Phenomenology*, Jean-Francois Lytopard
- Experimental Phenomenology: An Introduction, Don Ihde

- Introduction to Phenomenology, Robert Sokolowski
- Gestalt for Beginners, Sergio Sinay
- Gestalt Therapy and Human Nature: Evolutionary Psychology Applied, John Wymore
- Creative Process in Gestalt Therapy, Joseph Zinker
- Gestalt Therapy Integrated, Irv Pollster
- Joy: The Surrender to the Body and to Life, Alexander Lowen
- *Fear of Life*, Alexander Lowen
- *The Prince*, Machiavelli
- Fire in the Belly: On Being a Man, Sam Keen
- Anything and Everything, Joseph Campbell
- Unauthorized Freud: Doubters Confront a Legend, edited by Frederick Crews
- The Undiscovered Self, C. G. Jung
- *Blink*, Malcolm Gladwell
- *How We choose to be Happy*, Rick Foster and Greg Hicks
- Heinz Kohut and the Psychology of the Self, Alan M. Siegel
- Stress Management for Dummies, Alan Elkin
- Instant Relaxation: How to Reduce Stress at Work, at Home and in Your Daily Life, Deborah Lederer and Michael Hall
- The Mindfulness and Acceptance—A Workbook for Anxiety, John P. Forsyth and George H. Eifert
- Hurry Up and Meditate: Your Starter Kit for Inner Peace and Better Health, David Michie
- The Relaxation Response, Herbert Benson
- Transitions and Managing Transitions, William Bridges

Here's a computer program I wholeheartedly recommend:

• Healing Rhythms: Biofeedback Training for a Happy Mind and Healthy Body, Deepak Chopra, Dean Ornish and Andrew Weil

Here's a very useful training course I wholeheartedly recommend:

• The Breathing Box: Four Weeks to Healthy Breathing, Gay Hendricks

About the Author

Woody has been leading Gestalt style process groups for the past 10 years—focusing on the integration of mind, body and spirit. A self-acknowledged "educ-oholic," Woody holds degrees in physics, electrical engineering and materials science. When he isn't designing the next-generation cell phone battery charger or LED light bulb, you can find him taking courses in psychology, philosophy, Neurolinguistic Programming, Hypnotherapy, EFT and Reiki.

www.ingramcontent.com/pod-product-compliance
Lightning Source LLC
Chambersburg PA
CBHW022340280326
41934CB00006B/709